From MAR-A-LAGO *to* MARS

PRESIDENT TRUMP'S GREAT AMERICAN COMEBACK

NICK ADAMS

Skyhorse Publishing

Copyright © 2025 by Nick Adams

All Rights Reserved. No part of this book may be reproduced in any manner without the express written consent of the publisher, except in the case of brief excerpts in critical reviews or articles. All inquiries should be addressed to Skyhorse Publishing, 307 West 36th Street, 11th Floor, New York, NY 10018.

Skyhorse Publishing books may be purchased in bulk at special discounts for sales promotion, corporate gifts, fund-raising, or educational purposes. Special editions can also be created to specifications. For details, contact the Special Sales Department, Skyhorse Publishing, 307 West 36th Street, 11th Floor, New York, NY 10018 or info@skyhorsepublishing.com.

Skyhorse® and Skyhorse Publishing® are registered trademarks of Skyhorse Publishing, Inc.®, a Delaware corporation.

Visit our website at www.skyhorsepublishing.com.
Please follow our publisher Tony Lyons on Instagram @tonylyonsisuncertain

10 9 8 7 6 5 4 3 2 1

Library of Congress Cataloging-in-Publication Data is available on file.

Hardcover ISBN: 978-1-5107-8467-3
eBook ISBN: 978-1-5107-8468-0

Cover design by Brian Peterson

Printed in the United States of America

*To my mother and father:
the best parents a child could have ever hoped for.
You made everything possible.*

Contents

Introduction vii

Chapter 1:	A Presidential Precedent	1
Chapter 2:	MAGA Is Born	5
Chapter 3:	Tweet-Seeking Missile	11
Chapter 4:	2021: Courage in the Face of Darkness	19
Chapter 5:	Death, Loss, and Rebuilding in the Wilderness	29
Chapter 6:	The Moment of Truth	37
Chapter 7:	The Road to Renewed Greatness	47
Chapter 8:	Donald Trump: A Revolution in Language and Communication	55
Chapter 9:	The Rogan Republicans: Trade, Crime, and Inflation Wakes a Sleeping Beast	63
Chapter 10:	Podcasting the Presidency	73
Chapter 11:	The Greatest Mugshot of All Time	81
Chapter 12:	Trump: A Man of Tradition	89
Chapter 13:	Trump: A Man of the Future	103
Chapter 14:	Generation T	111
Chapter 15:	President of the World	119
Chapter 16:	Trump and Free Speech: My Mission to Make Trumpism Permanent	127
Chapter 17:	From TDS to DT Yes!	139
Chapter 18:	Trump's Effect on the Left	147
Chapter 19:	MAGA Meets MAHA	151
Chapter 20:	Election Night	157
Chapter 21:	President Trump's First Letter to the Future	161

About the Author 167

Introduction

I wrote this book with both an enormous sense of pride and the voice of American history whispering in my ear. I have stood beside President Donald Trump from the moment he declared his presidential candidacy in 2015. The journey has been one of Homeric proportions, but unlike Homer's poetry, it has a quintessentially American happy ending. Happily for us, I firmly believe that the best years of President Trump's time in the White House lie ahead for our great nation.

"Make America Great Again" has never been a mere slogan. It is a guiding force that makes me optimistic about our future, protective of our triumphant past, and on guard against those who would debase the currency of American exceptionalism.

President Trump represents the America I fell in love with as a child born in Australia—one touched by the greatness of the Reagan years. Beyond a shadow of a doubt, President Trump is not only the best president in my lifetime, but he is the finest since George Washington led the most noble revolution in the annals of world history.

This book is as much for future generations to learn about how it felt to be part of the greatest movement in American political and cultural history as it is for those of us here today who wish to understand what makes President Trump great, how he executes his great ideas, and all that he has already accomplished. It is a tale of where President Trump has been, where he is now, and about the road we now sojourn on together—as one nation under God.

I wrote this book at the dawn of America's New Golden Age. I believe it is my duty to ensure that this golden sun never sets on the land which was founded by those seeking freedom and made great by the blood and bravery of those who told us to "fight, fight, fight" for all that is good and true.

President Trump, thank you for saving the United States of America. I am forever indebted to you for the privilege of calling myself a proud citizen of this incredible nation!

Chapter 1

A Presidential Precedent

My support for President Donald Trump traces its origins to my teenage years. While it does not feel long ago, this was before *The Apprentice*, before social media, before the iPhone, and in my case, before America.

The year was 1998, and I was living in Australia, the nation of my birth. Even before that point, I had always loved and admired the United States. It was the land where dreams come true, where people think big, and where a man's destiny is in his own hands, so long as he is willing to work for it.

Some Americans reading this description of the United States may find it naive. Now that I am an American, I can understand why. For every Reagan, there is a Biden. For every JFK, there is an LBJ. But as someone who came from a country where the weather is nice, but the potential to live out one's personal dreams is slim, I have always appreciated that America at her worst is far better than any other country at its best.

A man like President Trump could truly only be produced in a country like the United States. From the moment I became acquainted with President Trump, I knew that he was a remarkable man with a great deal of wisdom to impart to anyone who would listen. My vision of President Trump, my aspiration to become an American, and my eagerness to strive beyond the world of my youth were the constituent elements of my own American Dream.

As a teenager in Australia, I had no opportunity to meet this larger-than-life figure, but on my thirteenth birthday, my best friend, Sanjay, gave me a copy of a book that would change everything. The book was *The Art of the Deal*, published in 1987 in the heart of the Reagan era when President Trump's real estate empire was creating a new era in New York City and beyond.

The Art of the Deal opened my eyes to new ways of thinking about success, manliness, intellect, interpersonal relations, and personal courage. Reflecting back on President Trump's consistency in his approach to all matters of business, from the business of real estate to the business of government, his book provides an honest and in-depth blueprint of the Trump way of getting things done.

From that moment forward I was on the Trump Train. I followed his interviews whenever I could see them, I read every article about him, and bought all of his subsequent books. Around one year after I first read *The Art of The Deal*, President Trump contemplated seeking the nomination of the Reform Party in the 2000 presidential election.

I was fascinated by this possibility. President Trump had long commented on politics, and this was the first time he seriously contemplated swapping the board room for the Oval Office. Ultimately, this flirtation with big-time politics proved to be short-lived due to President Trump's decision to withdraw from the nomination process of a small third party that lacked internal discipline and organization.

The late 1990s and early 2000s nevertheless proved to be a pivotal time for political outsiders at a gubernatorial level. In 1999, former professional wrestler Jesse Ventura became governor of Minnesota. Ventura shocked the world, first by winning an election and second, by becoming a competent, hard-working, and generally well-liked leader of his state. Of course, President Ronald Reagan was the first major leader to make the switch from the world of entertainment to the world of politics. But by the 1990s, due to President Reagan's advanced age, there were fewer and fewer Americans with direct memories of walking into a movie theater and seeing the Gipper on the big screen.

In November 2003, Arnold Schwarzenegger became governor of California. He was, of course, not the first actor to hold this position—that honor belongs to President Reagan. But like me, Schwarzenegger was not born in the United States—the possibilities seemed endless for someone watching this unfold.

Neither Ventura nor Schwarzenegger achieved anything close to the levels of political success that President Trump would, but from the vantage point of the turn of the twenty-first century, more and more people were asking whether President Trump would be the biggest political outsider of all time to conquer elected office.

During his interviews with Jay Leno and David Letterman from this era, the question almost always came up. The audiences clapped whenever it did.

Whether in his book or on television, President Trump had long presented detailed solutions to the many problems facing the nation. As fate would have it, the Obama presidency coincided with the launch of a little-known social media platform called Twitter. While Twitter's early features were unremarkable, even compared to other social media platforms of the time, there was one thing that made it the place to be.

In 2009, not long after Twitter's inception, President Trump began tweeting. While Twitter was initially conceived as a slightly enhanced form of text message, President Trump showed the world a new and novel way to use the platform.

Under President Trump's fingertips, a new way of communicating was born. Tweets were one part mini-press release and one part written sound bite. They offered a window into the world of public minds in real time, and in those days, without censorship.

While President Trump's professional life at the time was occupied by his real estate business, his other retail business ventures, and his top-rated television show, *The Apprentice*, there was something about President Trump's social media presence that hinted at something even bigger to come.

As the months and years rolled on, President Trump's tweets became increasingly political, increasingly critical of the Obama administration, and increasingly indicative of a future move into politics—this time, a permanent one.

By now, I was a frequent speaker at events across the United States. Thanks to President Trump's *Art of The Deal*, I made my way to the land of opportunity to live out my dream. By 2015, my activism and presence as a speaker and author within the Republican party and the wider conservative movement resulted in friendships with many elected Republican officials.

With the 2016 election around the corner, my big decision was this: Which one of my Republican friends running for president would I endorse?

Chapter 2

MAGA Is Born

In June 2015, everything changed. The man I had always wanted as America's president was running! From the moment President Trump and the beautiful future First Lady descended the golden escalator at Trump Tower to address a crowd of reporters and future MAGA supporters, politics would never be the same again, not for me, not for the nation, and not for the world.

President Trump's speech declaring his candidacy hit on all the key areas where America was suffering after nearly eight years of Obama. The fact that President Trump was able to articulate this with such clarity did not surprise me at all. I had been watching him closely for nearly two decades at that point.

What is stunning, in hindsight, is how prophetic the speech was. On that day, he said the following:

> Our country needs and deserves a comeback . . . but, we are not going to get that comeback with politicians. Politicians are not the solution to our problems—they are the problem. They are almost completely controlled by lobbyists,

donors, and the special interests—they do not have the best interests of our people at heart.

It is safe to say that President Trump really knew how to engineer both personal and national comebacks, more than anyone could have predicted at the time. His speech continued:

> The America we love will continue its decline because Washington is broken. We will never fix Washington from the inside unless we send someone to Washington from the outside. It is time for government to be run efficiently and effectively. It is time to get things done, and by done, I mean properly done! This is our time to once again make our government a government of the people, by the people and for the people. That is why today I am declaring my candidacy for President. I will Make America Great Again!

It is both pleasant and surreal to look back on that day when the phrase Make America Great Again was coined by the leader of a movement that would adopt this name as its moniker.

For me, the moment of decision came fast and easy. I threw my weight behind President Trump on that very day, and I never looked back. At the time, others told me I was foolish. I was advised to back one of the Republican candidates whom I knew personally, that it would boost my career in politics and lead to a bright future.

But I was raised to have principles and never surrender them for the illusion of short-term gain. Beyond this, I knew that President Trump was going to win. The message he conveyed from day one was the message that millions of Americans had wanted to hear for years. The people who did not want to hear the message were naturally those whose corrupt interests were immediately threatened by President Trump's commitment to the nation. The Washington insiders, the corporate lobbyists, the leaders of both parties, currency manipulators, foreign adversaries, and globalists were all in for a rude awakening.

There were two reasons that I knew President Trump was going to not only win the GOP primary but win the White House against the heir apparent of the Democrats, Hillary Clinton.

Firstly, President Trump had been waiting for his moment to lead his nation all his life. His media presence over the decades allowed him to lay out his vision for "Making America Great Again" with more clarity than anyone else in elected office or on the sidelines of politics. President Trump was always a man with a plan, and his business experience signaled to the world that he is someone who delivers on his promises—on time and under budget.

The other reason was my own experience with voters from across the country. Living far outside the Washington, DC bubble and the coastal media bubble gave me the opportunity to hear firsthand what voters felt was missing in every other political figure of the era. Politicians were seen as bland, insincere, self-serving, and more interested in serving the interests of those who sold the country out than those who had been sold down the river.

This is what I told the late, great Lou Dobbs when I appeared on his show on Super Tuesday of 2016. Following my introduction, Dobbs proclaimed something that went against the received wisdom of the time. Voters described as "moderates" were turning out for President Trump in big numbers.

I explained that the so-called experts would continue to be proved wrong because President Trump's message resonated and continues to resonate across our great, patriotic American middle class. Even in the midst of primary season, I proudly predicted that President Trump would "pulverize" Hillary Clinton at the polls. I saw it then, just as I see it now.

President Trump's vision for America is fully aligned with the hopes, dreams, and needs of the American people. While Dobbs responded that this is not what was reflected at the time in head-to-head polling, I explained that President Trump's appeal is neither transitory nor limited to a small but vocal base.

President Trump's appeal was and remains broad in its base and deep in its scope. To sum it up, I explained that Americans do not want a "butt kisser in chief" but instead they want a "butt kicker." I could see then that even the demure and wise Lou Dobbs had come to see that President Trump was the future. I'm proud to have ridden the Trump train with Mr. Dobbs. I just wish he could have seen the vindication of 2024.

At both a visceral and practical level, in President Trump, the people saw a man who was completely authentic in his personality and in his opinions. They also saw someone who represented a major threat to a status quo that was on the verge of making the American Dream extinct. When President Trump talked about bringing back the American Dream, the voters knew he meant it and could deliver.

In projecting greatness, President Trump inspires greatness in those touched by his message. That was the case for my teenage self after I read *The Art of The Deal*. It is likewise true of the Americans who would hear him speak throughout 2015, 2016, and beyond.

When I first endorsed President Trump, I did so without thinking our paths would cross, but I know that if they did, great things would happen. President Trump has an undeniably positive effect on people. For all of the wealth he has earned throughout his life, he has created exponentially more among all of those whom he inspires, assists, and mentors.

A journey like no other was about to begin for me, for President Trump, for our great nation.

Chapter 3

Tweet-Seeking Missile

More than any other year of my life, 2016 was a momentous year. It was the year that President Trump undeniably proved to the world yet again that anything he is told he cannot do, he is capable of doing. Critics were silenced, a corrupt media was stunned, the world was shocked, but most importantly, the American people were vindicated—President Trump was headed to Washington, DC.

In July of that year, I became a full-time US resident—helping to increase my own political activities, much of which revolved around campaigning for President Trump. Having a front-row seat at President Trump's first victory was something I would not have traded for the world. While the moon landing was before my time, and the fall of the Berlin Wall came when I was a small child, this was my generation's moment of truth, moment of triumph, and a moment of freedom's ultimate vindication.

Everything was now possible. While the legacy/fake media sounded the alarms of doom, the feeling among real people was one of optimism. All of a sudden, President Trump made politics important again. We no longer existed despite politics—politics was now something that could help to unleash our creative potential and usher in a new and more prosperous age of national dynamism and renewal.

President Trump's first inaugural address gave us the courage to articulate this bold new vision for America with clarity and purpose. As he stood on the steps of the Capitol, President Trump boldly proclaimed,

> Today we are not merely transferring power from one Administration to another, or from one party to another—but we are transferring power from Washington, DC and giving it back to you, the American People.
>
> For too long, a small group in our nation's Capital has reaped the rewards of government while the people have borne the cost.
>
> Washington flourished—but the people did not share in its wealth.
>
> Politicians prospered—but the jobs left, and the factories closed.
>
> The establishment protected itself, but not the citizens of our country.
>
> Their victories have not been your victories; their triumphs have not been your triumphs; and while they celebrated in our nation's Capital, there was little to celebrate for struggling families all across our land.
>
> That all changes—starting right here, and right now, because this moment is your moment: it belongs to you.
>
> It belongs to everyone gathered here today and everyone watching all across America.
>
> This is your day. This is your celebration.

> And this, the United States of America, is your country.
>
> What truly matters is not which party controls our government, but whether our government is controlled by the people.
>
> January 20th, 2017, will be remembered as the day the people became the rulers of this nation again.
>
> The forgotten men and women of our country will be forgotten no longer.
>
> Everyone is listening to you now.

While the reality of a Trump presidency is now part of both history and the daily life of Americans, during his first hour after being sworn in, there was a feeling that maybe it was all a dream. Was this really happening? Was it too good to be true? But there was the man whose book shaped my youth and helped guide me into adulthood, proudly proclaiming a new era where the people would no longer be ignored and left behind.

Minutes later, President Trump articulated the most central element of his political agenda, one he would have to deliver not once, but twice:

> We've made other countries rich while the wealth, strength, and confidence of our country has disappeared over the horizon.
>
> One by one, the factories shuttered and left our shores, with not even a thought about the millions upon millions of American workers left behind.
>
> The wealth of our middle class has been ripped from their homes and then redistributed across the entire world.
>
> But that is the past. And now we are looking only to the future.

> We assembled here today are issuing a new decree to be heard in every city, in every foreign capital, and in every hall of power.
> From this day forward, a new vision will govern our land.
> From this moment on, it's going to be America First.

As someone who fought my own battle to live in America and become an American, I am starkly aware of the fact that of all the things that makes this great country distinct from all others, is the social, economic, and cultural strength of the middle class.

The United States is a country where power resides in the nuclear family rather than in great halls of power. This is the case because the greatest middle class in history became owners of their own homes where they answered not to a bureaucrat, landowning corporation, prince, or tyrant but to themselves. Those who sought to undermine President Trump and mock his message were doing so because prior to his arrival in Washington, DC, the opponents of American greatness sought to weaken the country by weakening the middle class.

President Trump made it clear that the American middle class now had a powerful ally in the White House. Those who would come to tell Americans they would "own nothing and be happy," were in for the fight of their lives.

Not only did I make the right choice in endorsing President Trump from the beginning, I also correctly assessed that the mood of the American people was radically different than those in the halls of power who dismissed President Trump's history-making endeavour right up until the moment he declared victory on election night in 2016.

President Trump demonstrated early on in his first term that he wasn't just there to delegate; he was there to take a tireless and often thankless, hands-on approach to Making America Great Again.

When President Trump took the oath of office, many were asking whether he would "stop tweeting." Of course, the man who invented the use of Twitter as a means of mass communication was not about to hide behind bland press releases now that he was sitting in the Oval Office. Instead, social media became a form of statecraft, a way to instantly communicate policy decisions, resolve foreign disputes, and put domestic opponents on notice.

On March 3, 2017, President Trump's Twitter also became a powerful force that would change the history of *my* life. Up until that point, I had used Twitter more as a spectator than a participant, although that too was about to change.

On that day, I was invited to Fox News to discuss my book, *Green Card Warrior*. The book reflected both my journey to the heart of America, along with an analysis of the common-sense wisdom behind President Trump's immigration policies—policies that while extremely popular with the people, were a source of endless excoriation from the legacy media.

This was something of a transition period for me. I was still living in a rented two bedroom apartment in Grand Prairie, Texas, but now I was going home in the back seat of a Fox News limousine.

Suddenly, my phone started blowing up. Sometime between me leaving the studio and entering the limo, President Trump had tweeted an endorsement of my book. The entire world now wanted to speak to me. Was this what it felt like after winning on *The Apprentice?* In any case, what was clear was that President Trump's commitment to innovation and prosperity was not limited to rhetoric or even policies; President Trump was always willing to extend his hand to help those whose careers he felt were worthy of elevation. This was true about the man before he entered the White House, and it remains true to this day.

Around ninety minutes after I first heard about the tweet that would change everything for me, my father called and asked, "Have you thanked him yet?" I asked who he meant, and he replied, "The fucking president, you dickhead!"

"Oh shit, I haven't," came my reply. Ever someone to keep me on the straight and narrow, my father instructed me, "Stop everything you are doing and do it right now. RIGHT now."

To put things in perspective, at that time, I had only written around thirty tweets between 2009 and 2017. Because of my infrequent use of the app, I was not at all a seasoned tweeter and had to look up how to tag someone, respond, quote tweet, etc. As I was formulating my response and going back and forth on the precise language I wanted to use, the most incredible thing happened. I started getting notifications on my laptop screen from Twitter.com—@realdonaldTrump just favourited your tweet. @realDonaldTrump just favorited your tweet. @real Donald Trump just favourited your tweet. Four or five, in quick succession.

That is when it well and truly hit me—the president is on my Twitter page, going through each of my tweets, and liking them!

What tweets were they? Well, because I tweeted so sparsely, he was even liking tweets from 2013, going that far back. I will never forget the feeling. Having just become a permanent resident/ Green Card holder seven months earlier, sitting all alone on my Macy's couch with my laptop, in my rented two-bed, one-garage apartment, five minutes from the Dallas/Fort Worth airport—and here was the most powerful man in the world trawling through my tweets and liking them.

This feeling was a microcosm of the feeling of surprise, innovation, and renewal that President Trump had given the nation.

Literally anything can happen when President Trump is in charge. For me, it happened after he had only been in office for one full month. While my mind was focused on the big picture of how President Trump's multiple endorsements would forever change my personal American journey, it was also a moment to reflect on the tough love of my father, the man who made me who I am.

Later, on March 3, my father told me that I was able to "see further than he did." In other words, my choice to follow my dream to the land where dreams come true, no longer felt abstract and risky to my father. He was able to see, as it unfolded in real time throughout the day, that my hero, the leader of the free world, not only knew who I was, but that he supported and endorsed what I was doing.

Such a feeling can never be replicated. That was the moment I knew that everything I had done prior to this was training that would prepare me for the new chapter in my life. America was refreshed and so was I.

The night after being appointed to lead his nation, Winston Churchill said that he did not dream because "life was better than dreams." Now I knew what that meant.

As President Trump got America's economy firing back to life, in August 2017, he tweeted an endorsement of a previous book I authored, *Retaking America: Crushing Political Correctness*. It seems that he was a bigger fan than I realized!

It was then that I realized that decades before he knew who I was, and decades before I had even set foot on American soil, President Trump had mentored me. The words written on the pages of *The Art of The Deal* and his subsequent books had ignited something in me. I strove to emulate President Trump's refusal to take no for an answer when, inevitably, the small men of the world seek to crush your dreams. I learned to never give up and always believe that if something can be done, you must tell yourself, "I am the one who can do it."

While these lessons had a unique impact on me, they are lessons that everyone can and should take to heart. President Trump not only brought back the American Dream in an abstract sense. He made it very real for millions of Americans and continues to do so.

Chapter 4

2021: Courage in the Face of Darkness

Following the allied victory in the Battle of El Alamein at the end of 1942, Sir Winston Churchill said, "This is not the end. It is not even the beginning of the end. But it is perhaps the end of the beginning." For many reasons, this phrase helped to keep my head on straight during 2021, one of the darkest years in American political history.

Over six decades have passed since President John F. Kennedy's assassination, and although we understand more now than we did in the 1960s about the events of that day, significant mysteries and disagreements persist among those earnestly seeking the truth.

Just what happened during and immediately after the 2020 election may not be fully known for years. As early as February 2021, Molly Ball wrote a piece in *Time Magazine*, which proudly proclaimed a "conspiracy to save the 2020 election." By this, Molly means that forces external and unknown to the voting public worked to assure the outcome of the election before a single vote was cast.

Future books by future generations of forensically minded patriots will surely expose the full detail of what went on in 2020. Far more immediate to me at the time was the disloyalty I witnessed among those who had called themselves friends of President Trump. These were men and women who profited much from their relationship with the president. And yet, in a time that called for political unity, rhetorical solidarity, steadfast clarity of mind, and a calm attitude, the only image that comes to mind is that of rats deserting a floating ship.

I say floating ship, because Trump never lost his nerve, and never lost sight of his sworn duty to the American people. Other men would have thrown in the towel, others would have tried to cut sinister deals, and others would have simply become broken beyond repair. But not President Trump! In the darkest hours following the strange and alarming 2020 election, President Trump had a plan. His plan was to utilize little understood constitutional tools to assure that the "official" results of the election reflected the will of the people.

All of this was done while Trump continued to stoically carry out his presidential duties. While President Trump's strength shone brightly in difficult times, many in GOP circles were encouraging him to throw in the towel rather than seek the truth. This is the creed of losers and the strategy of fools.

Churchill said, "An appeaser is one who feeds a crocodile, hoping it will eat him last." In the days of January 2021, many of those who were already in the process of abandoning the president who sacrificed everything for his nation, were about to find out just how precise Churchill's analogy was and remains.

The morning of January 6, 2021, was a morning unlike any other. Everyone knew that President Trump was going to give a speech unlike any he had given before. He did not disappoint.

In his speech, President Trump directly accused big tech of conspiring to rig an election. This was before the *Time* article, which *credited* big tech executives with a "conspiracy" to assure the outcome of 2020. It was also before the lawsuits initiated by the attorneys general of Missouri and Louisiana that exploded mountains of evidence detailing a very real conspiracy of censorship between big tech and big government.

In his speech, President Trump blamed the media for fueling the big tech conspiracy. Subsequent data drops from the Twitter Files made it clear that old media was very much part of the drive by big tech and federal agencies to suppress free speech. Far from just talking about the aftermath of the 2020 election, President Trump's speech that day defended the legacies of American heroes including Washington, Jefferson, and Lincoln.

Since then, a statue of Thomas Jefferson was removed from New York City Hall, and the San Francisco Unified School District voted to remove the names Washington and Lincoln from multiple schools.

Thus far, everything Trump said in his speech turned out to be **true**.

Trump continued, criticizing the weakness of Republicans who were unwilling to advocate for the use of constitutional measures to assure that the election was fair. Just what were they afraid of? It turns out that they weren't afraid at all. They were more loyal to a system crafted by President Trump's opponents than they were to the People's Champ—President Trump.

Pundits operating on autopilot often talk about the need to put the country above party and this is just what President Trump did in his speech. President Trump observed,

The weak Republicans, and that's it. I really believe it. I

think I'm going to use the term, the weak Republicans. You've got a lot of them. And you got a lot of great ones. But you got a lot of weak ones. They've turned a blind eye, even as Democrats enacted policies that chipped away our jobs, weakened our military, threw open our borders, and put America last.

He later said,

Republicans are constantly fighting like a boxer with his hands tied behind his back. It's like a boxer. And we want to be so nice. We want to be so respectful of everybody, including bad people. And we're going to have to fight much harder.

In hindsight, it could be said that Trump was encouraging those supposedly on his side to "FIGHT, FIGHT, FIGHT." These, of course, were the words uttered by Trump following an attempt on his life in the months before the 2024 election. It can be said that in January 2021, President Trump was calling on others to display the same selfless courage that he always had within himself.

Far from a speech delivered from a place of anger, the president's speech was one of epochal strength in the face of the kind of political weakness that caused a majority of Republican voters to turn away from the old guard and embrace Donald Trump in 2015.

What happened next validated President Trump's indictment of his "fellow" Republicans. Following a riot at the Capitol, Democrats and their allies in the media and big tech rushed to amplify a narrative that a *speech* was responsible for what happened.

When I first heard this narrative, I found it hard to believe that anyone could believe such childish nonsense. The implication was that Trump was a kind of ancient siren bewitching sailors to crash their ships into the rocks. But this was the argument deployed by President Trump's political opponents.

The fact that Democrats and their corporate allies would spew such garbage was not entirely surprising. What was surprising was how Republicans did so little to counter this bogus narrative. This highlights a major problem running through conservative politics with the crucial exception of President Trump.

As someone who has delivered public speeches and participated in political debates beginning in my teens, I learned something that most of our conservative politicians have yet to grasp. He who defines the terms of the debate, controls the outcome of the debate.

In allowing the arguments surrounding January 6 to be framed by the Democrats, Republicans totally surrendered their opportunity to expose the absurdity that underpins the apparent supernatural linkage between rhetoric and riot. One could potentially forgive this stupidity, but if stupidity deserves grace, disloyalty most certainly does not.

When President Trump took charge of a new direction for the Republican party at the beginning of his first term, he was saving republicanism from itself.

Under President Trump, the Republicans went from being the party of Wall Street to the party of Main Street. It went from the party of managed economic decline to the party of economic revival and renaissance. It went from the party that participated in the degradation of our proud cultural traditions to one that proudly stood up for "Americanism not globalism," in the words of President Trump. Finally, it went from the party that followed Democrats into wars to one that lived by the credo of "peace through strength."

The ability of Republicans to win major elections in the twenty-first century is owed to President Trump and largely to President Trump alone. Did Republicans suddenly forget this in January 2021? Or did they instead revert to the pre-Trump mentality of political Stockholm Syndrome, where all they could muster was a defense of Democrat policies with a few bits of rhetoric about a road to inevitable national decline in which we would at least go the speed limit?

More than any of these ideological questions is one of personal values. What makes a man?

For me, the answer to this question has always been this:

Greater love hath no man than this, that a man lay down his life for his friends. —John 15:13-15

Without loyalty there can be no trust, and without a sense of interpersonal trust, suspicion gets in the way of getting things done.

Sadly, the Republicans fell into a doom cycle of disloyalty following the events of January 2021. In the words of Elvis Presley, "We can't go on together, with suspicious minds."

President Trump was well aware of this decades before the dark days of early 2021. In a 1992 interview with Charlie Rose, Donald Trump the businessman said the following:

> I used to say, and in fact I think I said in my first book and maybe this was foolish, but I really meant it, that someday I'd like to maybe lose everything for a period of time to see who's loyal and who's not loyal.

Rose then asked if Trump had found out who is and isn't loyal. Trump replied:

You can't guess it. You can't predict it. You think certain people would be loyal no matter what. It turns out that they're not. You just can't predict it. It's very difficult.

This was another of many Trump predictions that came true. I had a front row seat as many a would-be Brutus kicked Trump when he appeared to be down. But the truth is that Trump was never down.

President Trump left office after his first term much as he came in—a man on a mission to Make America Great Again. His final words as president in his first term were these:

I go from this majestic place with a loyal and joyful heart, an optimistic spirit, and a supreme confidence that for our country and for our children, the best is yet to come.

On President Trump's final day of his first term, I wrote the following to my supporters online. At the time, it felt mournful. In hindsight, it is a testament to the fact that loyalty to those who are loyal to us is the highest earthly virtue that we can attain:

Mr. President, what a ride it has been!

I supported you even back in 2012, and I was on the Trump train from June 16, 2015, when you announced.

I campaigned hard for you in 2016 and was honored to serve as a media surrogate for you in the 2020 election campaign.

In January 2017, I attended your inauguration, and all of the events surrounding it.

On March 3, 2017, less than six weeks into your Administration, I woke up one morning to discover I was on the front page of newspapers all around the world, after you tweeted about my book and national television appearance that you had watched. It was the first time a sitting President had ever endorsed a book.

On August 25, 2017, you did it again, endorsing another one of my books.

In mid-September 2017, I was able to fulfil [sic] a life-long dream—and not only visit the White House—but bring my parents there, too—as fitting a reward for the two people that had sacrificed so much for me, that I could ever muster.

In April 2018, I was able to host sixty people at the White House with tours and a chance to bowl at the Truman Bowling Alley at the White House. (Pictures attached).

In February 2019, I attended your State of the Union as a special guest.

In early 2019, FLAG was able to enter into a exclusive partnership with the White House to produce a student-friendly Constitution for children across America.

In the summer of 2020, you tweeted five more times about my newest book, with even fake news outlets having to admit I was "Trump's Favorite Author." Seven tweets in four years about three different books.

On July 2, Mr. President, you called me. The greatest honor of my life.

And then in early August, you gave me a Presidential appointment, giving me a fixed 6-year term on the Board of the Smithsonian. Again, 350 such appointments in a country of 350 million—truly a one in a million opportunity—and all at the age of 35. The stuff of dreams.

In September 2020, I was again able to host eighty of my patriotic supporters in the White House, making their own dreams come true.

You are a nice man—you didn't need to go out of your way to help a young Aussie immigrant—but you did—time and time again.

Mr. President, you were the greatest we ever had. You took on the world and tried to stop the fall of Western civilization. You were the only thing protecting them from us. Now we have no protection. The Chinese, the Islamists, the globalists, the eco-terrorists, the radical feminists, social justice warriors, corrupt corporates and censorious big tech overlords have no one to stop them.

Thank you for making my story and growing my American dream. Thank you for the indelible memories—memories I will carry for the rest of my life.

But more than anything, thank you for what you did for all of us, with everyone working against you and wishing the worst on you.

You are the ultimate patriot. You're an inspiration. America and the world didn't deserve you.

Despite facing betrayal of the worst kind, President Trump never let us down. The best certainly was yet to come, but before the world's greatest comeback, came the world's biggest effort to rebuild everything from scratch.

Chapter 5

Death, Loss, and Rebuilding in the Wilderness

While the final speech of President Trump's first term was filled with optimism and patriotism, a cold wind of un-American pessimism blew over the country just weeks earlier.

As the leader of the free world, the United States is a country that does not censor its people and does not try to control its history. At least it never did before 2021. When Orwell said "Who controls the past controls the future. Who controls the present controls the past," he may well have been talking about the ethos of big tech and the Deep State.

Checking President Trump's social media had become something of a daily ritual even before he took office for the first time. You wake up, have a large black coffee, and look at President Trump's social media. But on January 7, 2021, the unthinkable happened. Facebook, the biggest social media company in the world, censored the entire account of President Trump. A day later, Twitter, the platform that Trump helped to achieve its only profitable years, did the same.

A sitting president had been removed from public view in a clear attempt to both remove him from the public consciousness and more poignantly, to handicap his ability to defend himself against the 24/7 barrage of scandalous lies being told about him on the fake news media. This was something I never thought could happen in the United States. We're not Communist China or Stalinist Russia. When it did happen, I felt both sick and numb. How could we take America back from the tyrants of censorship who conducted a full-fledged digital coup against an elected leader?

When Air Force One flew out of Washington, DC to Florida with President Trump and First Lady Melania on board, the wolves of the fake news were jubilant in explaining that this was the "last time" anyone would see President Trump fly out of DC on that mighty aircraft. President Trump's supporters knew better; we knew that good guys can win in real life and not just the movies, and we knew that an America where anything is possible would always triumph over the anti-Americanism of censorship and stagnation. But at the time, few knew how we would begin to fight back.

When events of the world seem unknown or even unknowable, I always turn to the Bible. At that time, I was reminded of these words:

The Lord is nigh unto them that are of a broken heart; and saveth such as be of a contrite spirit. —Psalm 34:18

It was at this time that I temporarily lost touch with President Trump for the simple reason that I had always gotten in touch via the White House. Without social media, the wider public who did not know President Trump personally also lost touch, so to speak. The always open window into President Trump's mind, his humor, his wit, and his wisdom had been shut by the tyrants of Silicon Valley. Although difficult to locate, press releases would occasionally come out of Mar-a-Lago in the months following January 2021, but nothing was the same.

It was in March of that year that I faced the greatest loss of my life. This was a loss that every child eventually expects, but one for which we cannot ever be prepared.

Prior to 2021, the 3rd of March was always a happy day. In 2017, that was the day that President Trump first introduced me to the world via his Twitter account. It was the day that my father finally got to see that the greatest gamble of my life, coming to America and starting fresh, had paid off. The president of the United States was reading my books, he was tweeting about them, and he was heaping praise on my work.

Four years later, that was the day that I lost my father to that terrible virus from China.

Even though I was born in the 1980s, my father imparted an old-world discipline from another era. He was the man responsible for making me who I am. Until the moments before his death, my father never told me he loved me. He was from a generation and of a stoic mentality where such words did not need to be said. I never doubted his love.

Throughout my life, his love was shown through sacrifice, and through action. Just as President Trump always puts America First, so too did my father always put me first. The fact that my father was so hard on me was an expression of his love and care. At times he would be very hard, he would tear me down, but I later realized that he did this so that I would never falter and never fail when the *world* tried to tear me down.

President Trump's ability to remain strong and even optimistic when facing attempts to destroy him in every sense of the word, is surprising to many. A great number of men, tough men, find the president's unrelenting strength to be shocking in its indefatigability. But it does not surprise me. My father made me of stern stuff that President Trump likely received from his own great father, Fred. Such men create sons that are the opposite of "snowflakes," that are strong like a rock, mighty like a river, and unconquerable like the tallest mountain.

My parents were married for forty years. The vow "Til death do us part" was not merely a virtue to which one might aspire, it was the creed that bound them together from the first day until the sad loss of March 3, 2021.

During their marriage, they did *everything* together. My father was a good husband, in the sense of protecting and providing, but he wasn't a "date night and flowers" type of Hollywood romantic.

I think that what he was most proud of was being a father. As his son, I modeled myself on him in every way. I wanted to be as tall, as good looking, as smart, and as creative as him. But in my mind, I always fell short.

While he could be hard on me, I was always perfect in his eyes. From my earliest days as a public speaker, my father would be waiting for me the moment I left the stage. Invariably, there was always something I could have done better—a line or a phrase that could have been improved. He never hesitated to tell me right then and there how what I thought was my best, could have and should have been better.

My father was a genius and a strategist. I was his creation. This was a role I never failed to take seriously. If anyone wants to wonder where my confidence, passion, and resilience comes from, look no further than my father. These were the traits he instilled in me.

My father could have hardly predicted how social media would change human communication, but he knew that as Shakespeare said in *As You Like It*:

> All the world's a stage, And all the men and women merely players; They have their exits and their entrances, And one man in his time plays many parts, His acts being seven ages.

The stage is a place where there is no room for pausing, no time to gather your wits, no time to ask for a redo. The stage is here, and the stage is now. This is true of politics and in many ways, it is true of life. The United States might be the land of second chances, but it is also the place where the audience, the public, the crowd expects you to get it right the first time.

My father never treated me like a child. He treated me like a man. He spoke to men like a man, and he made it clear that I was to project the virtues of a man at a young age.

Our conversations were far more political than one might imagine. From an early age, he explained the perils of communism and collectivism, and he did not shy away from explaining the threats against Christian civilization. More than anything, he explained why conservatives struggle to win arguments and elections, a point that would be reiterated by President Trump in his speech of January 6, 2021.

When I began to reflect on the loss of my father, I began to examine just what greatness is within the confines of the human condition. I narrowed it down to four things. Some men are great husbands, some are great sons, some are great fathers, some are simply known as great men. I decided for myself that it would be my greatest aspiration to strive for, and my greatest honor to attain, the title of great son.

My parents sacrificed everything for me. They did not go on

vacations, so that I could travel as a child alone to Europe and see the old world as a traveler from the new. They did not drive luxurious cars, so that I could go far in life. They lived in a humble home, so that I might one day hold meetings in the home belonging to the president of the United States, Donald J. Trump.

I have used my own success to try to give back to my parents for all they have given me. While such a debt can never be repaid, I remember how proud I felt when I was able to upgrade my parents to first-class seats when they came to visit me in America.

And yet, it was not luxury that my father wished for himself. His joy came from seeing my success. His joy came from seeing that I was now living a life where fine dining, cold beer and wine at the ready, and a tennis court of my own were the status quo. I achieved these things not because my father gave them to me, but because he gave me the ability to achieve whatever I desired, so long as I was prepared to work like hell for it.

In the time when the end was drawing near, my father gave his last and potentially his best advice. He said that "life is short and you only get one shot at it. Go for it."

Our final ever earthly communication came in the form of a text message. I wrote to him, "I'm fighting with you and for you to the very end." He replied, "Don't worry about it, Nick. Get on with your work and have a great life, the best."

The next time we would be together was at his funeral at Saint Stefanos Greek Orthodox Church in St. Petersburg, Florida.

It is at the times when we feel most alone that we must turn to Jesus Christ, with whom we are never alone. While President Trump does not use the Cross for political purposes as many lesser men attempt to do, when he does mention religion, he does so with a profound understanding of God's oceanic power.

In the months following my father's death, I understood this feeling more than ever. While God rescued me from the emotional wilderness of paternal loss, I would have to FIGHT, FIGHT, FIGHT to make one thing very clear. President Trump's political career was not over, it was not even half-way over.

By the end of 2021, President Trump had taken it upon himself to reconnect with me. He would send me autographed printouts of my social media posts. Come December, President Trump ran into me at one of his speaking events with Bill O'Reilly as part of his *History Tour*. He said that it was good to see me. Somehow, I knew that everything would be all right.

At a time when most Republicans were floundering in the wilderness, I knew that the next three years would be spent alongside Trump, readying the greatest political and cultural comeback the world has ever seen.

The end of 2021 was also when I achieved another milestone. I had always been an American at heart and I believe also in deed. But now I was an American citizen. As the National Anthem so powerfully states,

> O say, does that star-spangled banner yet wave, O'er the land of the free and the home of the brave.

The America of 2021 felt neither free nor brave. But in America, anything is possible. This is what Making America Great Again is all about. We did it before, we would do it again.

When I became a citizen, I felt the blood of the patriots of 1776 flow through me. It invigorated and inspired me. I had achieved great things in my own life. President Trump achieved even greater things in his. But I knew that the best was yet to come.

It was my father who first introduced me to the courage and wisdom of Churchill. Just as there is a "Trump tweet" for every occasion, so too is there a Churchillism for every occasion. When Churchill proclaimed, "The pessimist sees difficulty in every opportunity. The optimist sees opportunity in every difficulty," he could have been talking about 2021.

Only in America could a song with the lyric "Don't stop believing, hold on to that feeling" become one of the biggest hits of all time. There is a good reason for this. America means never giving up.

For much of my life, detractors hoped I would give up. The media, big tech, and Deep State elites wanted Trump to give up in 2021. We would both show them otherwise, or to put it another way, we would tell them to GET BENT!

Chapter 6

The Moment of Truth

With 2021 safely behind us, it was now time to rekindle a spirit of optimism and innovation. In each of these areas President Trump delivered big. In hindsight, what President Trump accomplished in 2022 helped to pave the way for 2024 in ways that few could fully comprehend at the time.

In February 2022, President Trump boldly announced that he was back with the launch of the first major free speech driven social media platform: Truth Social. On February 16, Trump sent out his first Truth, telling the world,

Get Ready! Your favorite President will see you soon!

Suddenly, the world felt right once again. While the worst of Bidenflation was yet to come, now, President Trump was back talking directly to the American people without any fake news middlemen deconstructing and manipulating his language.

President Trump was the first major politician to successfully leverage the immediacy and pithiness of social media to get his points across without any filters. Whether challenging the hubris of foreign adversaries, putting arrogant "allies" in their place, or telling Congress what needs to be done, President Trump had used Twitter to successfully leverage a slow-moving political system that he forced to keep up with the fast pace of the twenty-first century.

Were it up to big tech and their leftist allies in the Deep State, President Trump would have been permanently deprived of this vital asset. President Trump had different plans.

One of the many areas where I feel a deep connection to the president is our shared ability never to take no for an answer. When someone says "it cannot be done" we work hard until we have developed a way to do it. When someone utters the phrase, "move on," we say, "move out of the way." When someone says, "better luck next time," we say that strong and determined men make their own luck.

In 1964, when addressing the Republican National Convention in San Francisco, Senator Barry Goldwater said,

> I would remind you that extremism in the defense of liberty is no vice. And let me remind you also that moderation in the pursuit of justice is no virtue.

At the time, Goldwater's robust defense of liberty at all costs sent shockwaves through a GOP establishment that was content to be the servants of someone else's destiny rather than masters of their own.

President Trump is a man who embodies Goldwater's words in everything he does. They are likewise words that I live by. When the freedom for which our country stands is on the line, when the very existence of the United States is on the line, anything and everything must be done to Make America Great Again.

At the beginning of 2022, this manifested itself with President

Trump's delivery of a promise to cut the cord from Silicon Valley and prove to the world that a successful social media platform can be launched and expanded without any help from the Boys by the Bay.

The creation of Truth Social sent strong reverberations through the rest of the tech world. First, Google and Apple had to concede that there was nothing they could do to prevent a well-built and totally secure platform from being listed in their app stores.

Second, the Trump Media & Technology Group's (Truth's parent company) partnership with Rumble helped to transform Rumble from an obscure video streaming platform to the go-to place for videos and streaming among those who value unfettered free speech.

Since partnering with President Trump's company, Rumble has become YouTube's only serious rival. This in turn has forced YouTube to roll back *some* of the more egregious forms of censorship that appeared on the Alphabet-owned platform prior to Rumble's emergence as a serious threat to the Silicon Censorship Cartel.

Third, after President Trump proved that free speech was in fact still possible online, Elon Musk grew increasingly frustrated with both the censorship, incompetence, and what he referred to as the criminality of Twitter.

Without President Trump's use of Twitter, even before he became president, it is doubtful that the platform could have ever become anything at all, not least because Facebook was always the superior platform for monetizing data and delivering targeted ads to users.

But Trump's use of Twitter prior to his disgraceful censorship off the platform helped the company to achieve the only two profitable years in its existence as a publicly traded entity.

By the time 2022 rolled around, the platform was bereft of its most popular user, who had moved on to the green pastures of Truth. Twitter was going to die due to a combination of corporate leadership as stubborn as stupid.

Luckily for those with large Twitter followings, myself included, Elon Musk acquired the company, took it private, and remade it into X, a new free speech platform whose ethos owes much to President Trump's pioneering creation of Truth Social.

As 2022 rolled on, President Trump continued to send more and more printouts of my social media posts with a personal message and signature.

Not only was President Trump back online in 2022, he was also back doing what he does best: holding the biggest and best rallies in the history of modern politics. Anyone who has ever been to a Trump Rally knows that these events are one part rock concert and one part Super Bowl. The energy is palpable, the air is electric, and the patriotism is undeniable.

For much of the year, President Trump's rallies weren't about him but about supporting Republican candidates in the midterms. While I did not throw my weight behind any specific candidate in the election, I was out there encouraging voters to go Republican across their ballots.

Although President Trump would not officially declare his intention to run for president a third time until after the midterms, anyone who attended even one of Trump's rallies in 2022 was well aware that he was the *only* candidate that the conservative and America First faithful were interested in.

The idea that any Republican would have the audacity to primary the most successful Republican since Reagan would have been unthinkable to the thousands of supporters who attended Trump Rallies from coast to coast.

Knowing this, I did not hesitate when a group of my supporters invited me to speak at a fundraising event for Florida Governor Ron DeSantis in June 2022. DeSantis, having been propelled into office due to President Trump's strong endorsement in 2018, was up for re-election, and as a Floridian, I agreed to drive across the state from my home in Tampa to Boca Raton in order to deliver a speech endorsing a second DeSantis term in Tallahassee.

The fundraising event took place poolside at the beautiful home of a local Republican donor. Although it was not a particularly sunny day, Governor DeSantis did not remove his dark sunglasses at any time during the event. Maybe I'm too old fashioned for my own good, but this immediately struck me. Something didn't feel quite right.

Duty bound, I delivered a powerful speech endorsing a second term for the Republican governor. What happened next reminded me of why I have always been and always will be a Trump supporter.

Following the speech, DeSantis did not shake my hand. He did not even acknowledge me. His wife was equally distant. Some of my supporters who invited me to make the speech asked the governor's handlers to pose for a commemorative photo with me. Although he agreed to do so, he never made good on his promise.

DeSantis left the event like a thief in the night. No real interaction, no warmth.

This event told me everything I needed to know about DeSantis. But more importantly, it reinforced everything I already knew about President Trump. Whether you're in a one-on-one meeting with Trump, a private fundraiser, or at a major rally in an arena, President Trump makes everyone in the room feel included, feel important, and feel like you're on a team captained by Trump himself.

President Trump is not only a charismatic speaker, but he is a great listener. During my private meetings with the president, he listened to my every word—I could see the wheels turning in his head. His responses are based on the issue at hand, not some pre-programed sound bite. President Trump is both a quick thinker and a quick doer.

Perhaps even more important is that President Trump will do anything and everything to make sure that his audiences feel that they are included and that their presence is valued. I have never seen President Trump turn down a request for a photo. In each photo he poses for, whether with a Senator, surrogate, or ordinary supporter, his effervescent smile and sincere enthusiasm is palpable.

It is not just at political events where President Trump goes the extra mile to make sure that everyone feels included. When President Trump is present during a major event held at one of his properties, he will always make the effort to introduce himself to the people at the event and make sure that everyone is having a good time.

Whether playing host at a Trump hotel or resort or rallying the voters, Trump is aware that while he is one of the wealthiest men in the world, good manners cost nothing. I take this to be another indication of the president's upbringing, one that as I have said, is surprisingly similar to my own. Self-discipline must never come at the expense of anti-social tendencies.

Always look people in the eye during a conversation. Express gratitude even when you are the star. Keep your handshake firm. Be a good host. Receive praise with grace. Most of all, a smile is always more compelling than a scowl.

To this day, I have no idea whether DeSantis is habitually ill-mannered, has poor political instincts, or is just ill-prepared for the personal elements of a major public-facing position in politics.

What I do know is that when President Trump gave the Florida governor a new nickname on the eve of the midterms, I knew exactly why.

At a rally five days before the midterms, President Trump addressed a poll of hypothetical primary challengers in the next presidential election. While DeSantis had yet to confirm *or deny* rumors that he would selfishly abandon his gubernatorial position to run for president, many "Never Trumpers" were already privately encouraging him to betray the man who put him on the political map.

When reading the poll, Trump smiled while proclaiming that his numbers were better than those of "Ron DeSanctimonious." After seeing the governor's holier than thou attitude up close and personal, I knew that like all of the president's classic nicknames, they are based on reality. Once you get a Trump nickname, you'll never shake it. From now till eternity, it will always be Cooked Hillary, Crazy Nancy Pelosi, Pocahontas (sometimes known as Elizabeth Warren), Sleepy Joe Biden, and yes, Ron DeSanctimonious.

President Trump did not only change the history of the world, he changed the way that politicians speak. Prior to President Trump, most political figures communicated in a dull, bureaucratic, and uninspiring dialect that was entirely removed from reality. Such politicians dealt in euphemisms intended to beguile the public.

But President Trump introduced a new way of communicating, one that is direct, inspirational, clear, concise, memorable, humorous, witty, and above all, masculine. A Trump speech has balls, and the man has the policies to back up the rhetoric.

While most politicians pretended to be shocked and horrified by Trump's manly mannerisms, the public loved it. Even Trump's opponents can't help themselves when they unconsciously integrate Trumpisms into their rhetoric.

Today, everyone tries their best to sound like Trump even though most fail miserably. Rhetoric with conviction must come from the heart. You cannot fake it. Some of us never have to try. You're either born with it or you are not. It's a small club and most politicians just aren't in it. Be that as it may, thanks to Trump there are fewer multisyllabic euphemisms in American politics and there is more direct language.

Even so, a number of Republicans criticized Trump for giving a Republican governor from a large state a nickname on the eve of the midterms. It turns out that Trump knew what we later all found out. While it might be possible to win elections while being sanctimonious by the poolside, such an attitude doesn't win votes where it counts.

Modern elections are won and lost not on the coasts, and not in the south—they are won and lost in the Midwest.

The Midwest is the engine of productivity that transformed the United States into the leading economic powerhouse of the world by the turn of the twentieth century. Even before the industrialization of the Great American West, our country was built on the shoulders of Chicago and Detroit.

Democrats have left these great cities in a terrible state, while voters from rural Ohio to factory towns in Wisconsin and Indiana look to President Trump to restart the stalled engine of American productivity.

I knew at the time that DeSantis, sunglasses and all, was not going to convince Midwestern voters that he is on their side. As such, a DeSantis led Republican presidential ticket was going to lose, no matter how bad the Democrats are. President Trump understands how to make our Midwest Great Again, DeSantis did not. It was the biggest open and shut case of electoral realism in history.

I knew also that President Trump not only could but *would* win in 2024. A week after the Midterms, President Trump put his cards on the table. He was now officially in the race to return to the White House.

In 2023, I would speak with President Trump about my plan to help him get there.

CHAPTER 7

THE ROAD TO RENEWED GREATNESS

I spent Thanksgiving of 2022 with President Trump. Following the declaration of his intention to run in 2024, it was all hands on deck. Less than two months later, I was visiting Sydney, Australia when I noticed that I had several missed calls from a number in Palm Beach.

I knew it was the president. Owing to time zone differences, I wasn't able to connect directly but on the January 7, 2023, President Trump left me a voicemail congratulating me on a speech of mine that he saw on C-SPAN.

I hadn't even made it onto my plane stateside before I got another call from President Trump. Two days after the voicemail, I was at Sydney airport about to board a flight to Los Angeles. As I was checking in at the check-in counter, after I had already handed over my passport, I got a call from the 561 Palm Beach number I had come to know as "the" Palm Beach number.

Not wanting to miss this important call, I apologized to a not very understanding young female Qantas agent, and over her protestations (in fairness, there was a long line behind me and we had already begun interacting), I answered the call.

I said to her, "You don't understand, I have to answer this call. It's the president of the United States calling." Her eyes darted everywhere, and I could tell she contemplated for a split-second calling security. I answered the call and was greeted by an ebullient Trump. For about three seconds as he was greeting me, I put it on loudspeaker to prove my point. She just about fainted.

When she came to, she started telling the other agents on either side at her neighboring counters who I was on the phone to. The president asked me how I was, where I was, when I was coming back, told me how great I was on TV, and he told me to please come and see him when I came back. As I got off the phone, I apologized again. The agent, called Avalon, had gone from suspicious to admiring. She said, "Who are you???" I said, "No one special."

"Yes, you are," she replied, "you're getting a phone call from the president of the United States. I'm just a normal Aussie girl. I had my Weet-bix this morning. This is the wildest thing that has ever happened to me on the job here."

Not one to miss the opportunity, given she was attractive, I asked for her name and number! Trump is not only good for the career but love life, too!

The next month, on February 9, I returned to Mar-a-Lago for a deeply important private meeting with the president. Now that primary season was around the corner, we needed a game plan, not just for victory, but for a victory that was "too big to rig."

My meeting with the president took place at a time when the GOP and the wider conservative world was in the midst of a major identity crisis. Loyalties were being tested, and new political battlelines were being drawn.

Going into 2023, President Trump was up against an astroturfed narrative which falsely claimed that his brand had become "too toxic" for the general election. This narrative further implied that because of this, it was the "duty" of Republican voters to select someone who would represent "Trumpism without Trump."

I knew from the start that such a notion was a steaming pile of excrement. The British Prime Minister Harold Wilson once said that "a week is a long time in politics." This might explain why nothing is shorter than the political memory of the people working against you.

Luckily, I remembered that in 2015, it was not Trump *the man* that incurred the exclusive ire of the RINO faction of the GOP, it was also Trump *the policy revolutionary* that angered them so.

The RINOs of 2015 said that tariffs would collapse the economy. Of course they were wrong, and we had the best economy ever under President Trump.

The RINOs of 2015 said that Trump would start a world war. They couldn't have been more wrong, President Trump was the only president in decades not to start a new war while making historic peace in the Middle East and Northeast Asia.

The RINOs of 2015 said that by ending NAFTA and bringing heavy industry back home, President Trump would destroy manufacturing, instead he began a long overdue revival in good American jobs for the long neglected American working man.

In everything the RINOs of 2015 said about President Trump's policies, their "predictions" were not just wrong, they were antithetical to the record of supreme achievement that was a hallmark of the first Trump administration.

The fact that the president was able to accomplish this with his hands tied behind his back by the Deep State and disloyal members of his own administration, is a further testament to the fact that you simply can't stump the Trump.

In our meeting, I explained my particular view of the lay of the political land. Trump soberly asked me, "So, let's talk about this great political comeback—what do you think I need to do?" I declared, "Mr. President, it's all about the men. Young men, in particular. You've got to drive them out in record numbers." Trump looked at me quizzically. He said, "It's a good demographic for me, right? I do pretty well with them." Without hesitation, I replied, "Yes, Mr. President, but this time we are going to go after them like no campaign has ever gone after them before. Because they'll win you the election."

For all the funny business associated with the corrupt 2020 election, one thing was clear, President Trump won more votes than any Republican in history up to that point. In that election, President Trump expanded his vote among women, Hispanic Americans, Asian Americans, and among Black Americans. These are achievements of which President Trump is justifiably proud. But there was a problem. While Trump's campaign team worked tirelessly to expand the big tent coalition of voters that rallied to Trump in 2020, the emphasis on the male vote in general, and the young male vote in particular, was lacking.

In the previous chapter, I made it clear that all modern elections are won or lost in the Midwest. The male vote in these Midwestern swing states is vital to winning the electoral vote, and in particular, the young male vote turning out in high numbers is essential to winning a popular mandate.

In order to win an election that was "too big to rig," it was clear that we would not only need a strong electoral college victory, but we would also need to secure the popular vote. This meant that the young male vote was essential.

I told President Trump that what was missing in 2020 was strong messaging directed to men. Such messaging needed to let male voters know that there is someone who understands their hopes, someone who is sympathetic to their fears, and someone who is there to tell them that it is okay to laugh at the absurdity of wokeness, the feminization of discourse and the corporate love affair with disgusting degeneracy.

The American male and in particular, the white American male, is the most maligned of all demographics. While this is the demographic that founded the United States in 1776, the heirs to this great tradition are immersed in the propaganda of self-loathing from the moment their communist public school teacher begins yapping about "colonialism," "white privilege" and other made-up concepts.

But far from being detached from the great works and deeds of their forebearers, today's American male is made to feel undeserving of the basic living standards that just a generation ago were taken for granted. Just due to being a white, heterosexual male, twenty-first-century America closes doors in your face whether these doors lead to educational opportunities, employment opportunities, opportunities to influence others, and even opportunities for entrepreneurialism.

This anti-American crusade against male greatness, which began in late twentieth-century San Francisco, had infested the country like a plague under the leadership of Barack Hussein Obama.

This anti-male hatred ended up causing some young American men to develop a peculiar and pathetic defense mechanism. Instead of fighting back against the mechanisms of feminized Marxism, I began to see far too many young males begin to accept the "reality" that they are worthless, that they should feel lucky to be able to breathe the same oxygen as a diverse lesbian self-identifying female of color, and that if they have any role in the new America, it is to dutifully serve the corrupt Sheocracy.

In 2016, these men said, "Hell no, we won't go quietly into this undignified night." They expressed this sentiment by casting their vote for President Trump.

Their reasons are not uncomplicated. In an age where even older men in politics, corporate America, and legacy media have feminized their manner of speech, gone out of their way to appear less intelligent than they are, and adopted tones more associated with a female managerial class who attained their positions through pathos rather than skill, President Trump struck a literally different chord.

President Trump isn't afraid to tell it like it is. He doesn't shy away from telling a loser that he is a loser. He isn't afraid to call big fat Rosie O'Donnell fat. He isn't afraid to call Joe Biden stupid. He isn't afraid to tell America's "allies" that they have been ripping us off for decades.

President Trump can be dignified and gallant, but he can also be conversational, realistic, and pragmatic. It is this second rhetorical talent of President Trump that won the support and confidence of a generation of men who were told to suppress their instincts and be something they are not.

Not only does President Trump lead young men to embrace their natural tendencies, more importantly, he inspires them to achieve greatness. In order to do this, you must want something more, you must desire to be something more, and in order to make this happen, you must work perpetually to make the dream of greatness come true.

These conversations formed the central theme of our meeting. We also discussed my plan to include many of these themes in a book aimed directly at young males. President Trump loved what

I was going for in my then-unwritten book which would go on to be called *Alpha Kings*.

President Trump understood that if young males can be inspired to stare a rigged system in the face and say, "not this time, partner," they would grow up to be the strong, unshakable masculine individuals who would never fathom voting for anyone other than Donald J. Trump.

After our serious talk about the winning strategy to bring back young men to the Trump fold *en masse*, President Trump, who is always full of pleasant surprises, picked up his desk phone.

A minute later, I was in the middle of a three-way conversation with none other than Sylvester Stallone. Unlike many of today's on-screen fruitcakes, Sly Stallone has always been a man's man. More than that, he has never compromised on his creative vision. He refused to allow studio pressure to water down the script he wrote for the first *Rocky* film. He also knew that no other actor could play Rocky. It was a role that he alone was *born* to play.

So there I was on a three-way phone call with two of the most stubbornly successful men of our age, albeit from two very different backgrounds. What President Trump and Sly Stallone had in common was a unique confidence that was backed up by excellence. This is something I have always striven for—it is a lesson in character handed down to me from my father.

While I've never been a fly on the wall during any meeting held by Sleepy Joe Biden, I can't imagine a scene unfolding before Sleepy Joe that involved a patriotic American who happens to be from Australia, Rambo, and the Club Champ who happens to be the best president ever, all shooting the breeze while planning the greatest comeback of all time. Then again, I can't think of a better team to launch just such a comeback.

Game on!

Chapter 8

Donald Trump: A Revolution in Language and Communication

Everyone now admits that President Trump changed politics forever, but it is well worth exploring the specific ways in which he brought about such profound change. Perhaps this change is no more noticeable than in the ways that President Trump changed the very way politics is conducted at the level of rhetoric.

In one of his most memorable stand-up routines, the very non-right wing comedian George Carlin said,

> I don't like words that hide the truth. I don't like words that conceal reality. I don't like euphemisms, or euphemistic language. And American English is loaded with euphemisms. Because Americans have a lot of trouble dealing with reality. Americans have trouble facing the truth, so they invent a kind of a soft language to protect themselves from it, and it gets worse with every generation. For some reason, it just keeps getting worse.

Prior to President Trump, politics seemed to be the womb from which this soft euphemistic language emerged. The people that complain about President Trump's use of rhetoric can be classed as those who prefer lies and obfuscation over straightforward truth. For instance, pre-Trump, a Republican might refer to an incompetent liberal governor as "someone with whom we must work to explore the possibilities of compromise." This means absolutely nothing in the *real world*.

For President Trump, such a governor is "stone cold incompetent."

Before President Trump, "Although we contribute far more to NATO than our allies, we nevertheless value them as equal members of a vital group fighting for democracy." Fighting how? With what?

Under President Trump, "We have many NATO members that aren't paying their bills, and you can't forget about that. You can't say, 'Well, let's take care of this.' You have to say, 'Folks, if you don't pay your bills, you get no protection.' It's very simple."

It is very simple, yet prior to Trump, our political class was collectively fearful of speaking the truth.

Under President Trump, those with a "uniquely bespoke appearance" were back to being called "ugly." Those with a "highly active nutritional intake" were back to being fat. Those who were "pugnacious defenders of radical feminism" were back to being a "degenerate" and "slob."

"Our congressional friends who have a different understanding of political realities" were back to being "liars." China was beating us because our side was "stupid." And OPEC's days of taking advantage of us ended when President Trump told them, "You're not gonna raise that fucking price, you understand me?"

During the final days of the 2024 campaign, at a rally in

Milwaukee, President Trump devoted around twenty minutes of his speech to slamming a poorly assembled microphone stand on his lectern. It was twenty minutes of utter brilliance. The humor, the realism, the important subtext about how every job worth doing is worth doing well. If you wonder why President Trump has been so successful in both business and politics, you can learn a great deal by watching him complain about the faulty mic stand.

Rather than take these lessons to heart, predictably humorless leftists decried President Trump as someone "unfit for office" because of his rant about the microphone stand. What such people lack is both an imagination and contact with reality. If you are a strong, masculine man in a leadership position, you do not just assume perfection, you expect it. When those around you fail, you let them know just how bad the failure is.

They either improve or they take a hike. That is how great coaches like Vince Lombardi, Tom Landry, Chuck Noll, and Bud Grant drilled discipline into their players. But President Trump is not just a narrow disciplinarian. He is also someone who can deploy wit, sarcasm, and other forms of biting humor to get a point across. Here too, there are examples from football.

Coach John Madden never cared what his team did off the field so long as they showed up on time and played like hell. Madden had a saying, "Don't worry about the horse being blind, just load the wagon." This quote is all about results. Get the job done. Don't stop to ponder about the various ways a good job can be done, in the time it takes a lazy person to contemplate, a doer has already found the best way by getting his hands dirty in the real world.

But President Trump is *even* more than someone who inspires discipline, and action. He is also someone with an attention to detail that only those who have met with him one-on-one can truly appreciate. In 2024, voters had an opportunity to see this side of President Trump more than ever before, thanks to his appearance on multiple long-form podcasts, including *The Joe Rogan Experience*.

In this sense, he can be compared to the professorial coaches who changed the game by throwing it wide open to innovation. Men like Paul Brown, Don Coryell, Joe Gibbs, Bill Walsh, Mike Marz, and yet again, Tom Landry.

But President Trump's virtues do not end there. He is also someone who can think on his feet, changing direction when the reality on the ground changes. Like a great general, he knows that there is not *a* way to win, but rather there are *ways* to win. It's the winning that counts more than anything. This too recalls an analogy from football. In 1972, coach Don Shula achieved the only perfect season to include a Super Bowl victory. He did this with a relentless ground game featuring the likes of Larry Csonka and Mercury Morris. But by the eighties, the game had changed. Shula found himself with one of the best pure pocket passers of all time, a young man from Pittsburgh named Dan Marino. Shula developed a game plan that would allow Marino to play to his strengths. The team became defined by a wide-open passing attack as a result.

President Trump not only is able to think on his feet in terms of policy decisions, but also in his manner of speech. It is accurate to say that if you can speak on your feet, you can also think on your feet. No one is more quick-witted than President Trump. There are enough examples of this to fill a book, but one of his best improvisational moments came during a White House press conference when he called on ABC News reporter Cecilia Vega to ask a question.

Noticing that she did not expect to be called, President Trump joked, "She's shocked that I picked her. She's in a state of shock. That's okay."

Feeling somewhat bewildered, Vega said, "I'm not thinking, Mr. President."

Quick as a flash, President Trump rerouted, "I know you're not thinking, you never do."

Even if Vega was preparing to ask the most scathing and insulting question of all time, it would not have landed after that. President Trump's wit totally disarmed the stiff and unthinking reporter.

Long before Joe Rogan had President Trump on his podcast, he referred to the president as someone who possessed better rhetorical and intellectual timing than most of the best stand-up comedians. In another universe, President Trump could well have been on stage at a comedy club, bringing the house down every night. He is just that good at coming up with a zinger when the room needs one.

In bringing truth and humor back to politics, President Trump has made politics matter more than ever before to the average American. In the early 2000s, I recall bloated leftist Michael Moore complaining of political apathy among young voters. President Trump fixed this problem, and I played a role in getting young male voters onto the Trump train. The kind of enthusiasm President Trump inspires is something that you would think might be universally praised.

Of course, when the leftists talk about ending apathy and getting out the vote, they are only referring to those who vote for Democrats. President Trump challenged the assumption that only charismatic radical leftists can cure voter apathy. As early as 2015 when Crooked Hillary forced Crazy Bernie out of the election, many Sanders supporters switched not to *her* but to President Trump.

Although Sanders is a man of the old left and President Trump is the creator of the modern right, it should not be hard to understand why this happened. Bernie offered young people hope. He railed against corruption and said that he would be on their side.

President Trump likewise exposed corruption in far more moving language than Bernie could muster. He also gave young people hope and pledged to be on their side by Making America Great Again. While some of these young people switched from Bernie to President Trump as a means of sticking the middle finger to the face of a rotten establishment, over time, I have seen firsthand how President Trump's first administration educated many of these people about the specific virtues of his policies.

By creating the best economy ever, and by doing so with a unique charismatic flair, young people began to realize that big government can never be on their side, but cuts to regulation can create an environment where fresh ideas can thrive and become profitable.

President Trump showed young voters that when you apply common sense to world trade, you can stand up to bullies and achieve a fair and honest outcome. President Trump also showed young skeptics that it is never impossible to rebuild that which was lost. Everyone assumed NAFTA would be there forever, but President Trump killed it off forever and replaced it with a USMCA that puts American jobs and patriotic American business first.

Without President Trump, I cannot see how the GOP would have had any success in general or midterm elections following the Obama years.

Instead, President Trump expanded the appeal of the right by giving people real opportunity for real success. While hope is a promise, it soon turns to hopelessness when not backed up by hardline actions.

President Trump delivered and because of his linguistic honesty, millions of Americans knew who was responsible for making things better than ever. This was a towering achievement, but President Trump's words and deeds would go on to consecrate an even more revolutionary change to electoral politics and governance in 2024.

CHAPTER 9

THE ROGAN REPUBLICANS: TRADE, CRIME, AND INFLATION WAKES A SLEEPING BEAST

President Reagan is remembered as the most popular Republican leader of the twentieth century. I grew up as an ideological child of the Reagan revolution and embraced his optimistic spirit that was implicit in his policies that helped to unleash an economically forward-thinking America while assuring the public that traditional values were not extinct—they simply needed to be renewed.

In each of Reagan's sweeping victories, a phenomenon was observed of lifelong Democrat voters who cast their vote for Reagan in both 1980 and even more so in 1984. This broad cohort was named "The Reagan Democrats." It is no coincidence that this cohort was initially observed in Michigan, a key state that President Trump definitively won in his two affirmed electoral victories.

Whether our coastal elites wish to admit this or not, the Midwest is the beating heart of modern America. It has been since our industrial revolution. Even President Reagan was not fully equipped to stand up to the many political forces that weakened our Midwestern economic dynamism in the false name of "free trade."

Through a combination of political foolishness and geopolitical naivety, our great Midwestern industries were sold out over many decades. Long before his entry into electoral politics, President Trump identified these problems and proposed realistic, patriotic solutions.

The phrase "free trade" naturally appeals to many Americans. As people who have benefited from the greatest Constitution ever written, we are naturally sympathetic to the impulse for freedom, irrespective of where and how it might arise. As a nation of enterprise, commerce, and innovation, we likewise understand the importance of both domestic and international trade.

But just as our heroic men in uniform understand that freedom isn't free when it comes to matters of life and death, it is likewise the case that free trade is neither free nor does it involve trade-offs that any rational person would consider fair.

On September 2, 1987, President Trump made one of his many appearances on CNN's *Larry King Live*. When asked about the free trade conundrum, he said the following,

> I believe it's very important that you have free trade. But we don't have free trade right now, because if you want to go to Japan, or if you want to go to Saudi Arabia or various other countries, it's virtually impossible for an American to do business in those countries. Virtually impossible. Now I have many friends, they go over to Japan, they can't open up anything. They need approvals, they need this,

that. In the meantime, Japan comes over to this country, they're buying up Wall Street, they're buying up all of Manhattan's real estate, they're buying—which is fine as far as I'm concerned because they're paying premium prices that put people like myself in a very good position—if I ever want to sell something. So, the fact is that you don't have free trade. We think of it as free trade but you right now don't have free trade.

Substitute Japan, the Asian economic powerhouse of the 1970s and 1980s, with China, the Asian economic powerhouse of the early twenty-first century, and literally everything President Trump said in 1987 was and remains true regarding our present trade problems.

Adding to the problems of so-called "free trade" is the fact that many of the countries with which we trade freely, are subsidized by the American taxpayer. Thus, we are paying twice for the same goods. We first subsidize the defense of these countries and then contented with buying goods from their protected industries while we refuse to protect our own.

President Trump has always understood and articulated that our great industry was built on tariffs. In the nineteenth century, our industrial revolution would not have been possible without tariffs. We protected and supported our industries, and by the presidency of William McKinley in the 1890s, American industrial output was the largest in the world. This was not only a time of high tariffs, it was a time of zero income tax, low regulation, no Federal Reserve, and the classical gold standard. As a result, the period in question was a sustained golden age of American greatness.

Because no single economic instrument can be used in isolation, in addition to understanding the overarching benefits of tariffs, President Trump also understands that tariffs and all they entail are far preferable to the American family when compared to the disastrous income tax that should have never been enacted in the land of the free.

The permanent political class, including both the Deep State and many of our brain dead politicians, globalist economists, and those who prioritize short-term ease over long-term domestic growth, still do not comprehend that tariffs have a great dual utility, both as a direct means of protecting the economy and as a major weapon in our diplomatic arsenal that can be used to achieve good deals with both adversarial nations and our many two-faced foreign "partners."

In the same Larry King interview, President Trump identified the unfair reality of other nations taking advantage of America's short-term thinking on trade,

> I think that people should make a contribution, and a major contribution—other countries—to this country for what we're doing to keep their freedom, and to keep them free, and to allow them to be free. And would you rather have that, or would you rather see this country go totally bust in another couple of years, because this country cannot afford to defend Japan and every other country in the world? It just cannot afford it.

He added, "I think that Japan and all of these other countries should certainly pay. They can well afford to pay."

In this eye-opening interview, President Trump also decries insufficient means of protecting the dollar against foreign nations that manipulate their currency to make their exports artificially deflated in terms of cost to the American consumer. While this might appear to be beneficial to the American consumer in the short term, the long-term effect was the collapse of many vital industries which in turn led to unemployment. This naturally leads to the collapse in American purchasing power. It's a losing game and for too long, our politicians were willing to play it.

In 1999, President Trump explored the possibility of running for president as a member of the Reform Party that had seen success under Ross Perot, a man who warned of many of the same problems identified by President Trump.

In 1992, Perot opposed the creation of the North American Free Trade Agreement (NAFTA). In expressing his opposition to NATO, Perot warned of a "giant sucking sound"—a metaphor for the jobs being sucked out of the country and into Mexico and Canada. Perot's Republican and Democrat opponents each championed NATO. President Clinton ended up creating it. President Trump, in his first term, brought it to an end.

Like Perot, President Trump was a successful businessman. There is no doubt in my mind that a theoretical understanding of economics and trade, without real world experience to underpin such an education, is as useless as trying to teach calculus to a wombat.

In 1999, President Trump reiterated many of the same policies he advocated in 1987. Speaking to Larry King that year, President Trump said,

> What you can do is you can negotiate fair trade agreements. So that instead of billions and billions of dollars going out, you can reduce your taxes by having it come back in. You know, I know the best negotiators. I would put the right people in charge of negotiation. We've been

ripped off as a country by virtually every country we do business with.

Outlining his continued opposition to NAFTA, President Trump said,

> The reason NAFTA looks OK now is because the economy is strong, but when the economy is not strong, which, unfortunately, will at some point happen, NAFTA is going to look like a disaster.

He continued,

> I'm not an isolationist. What I am, though, is I think that you have to be treated fairly by other countries. If other countries are not going to treat you fairly, Larry, I think that those countries should be—they should suffer the consequences.

This is the essence of the Trump view on trade. When you have unfair deals that are negotiated unwisely or worse yet, in bad faith, America gets screwed. This means that factories close, jobs are lost, and national security is harmed.

During the global shutdowns of 2020, many consumers and small business owners experienced firsthand just how over-reliant we are on global supply chains. To put it bluntly, we are reliant on the good graces of dishonest leaders in countries that either dislike us or actively oppose us.

Two months to the day after 9/11, China formally joined the World Trade Organization (WTO). This was a move supported by most elected officials from both major parties. It was opposed by

President Trump. At the time, he called it one of the worst mistakes we could make. This position, which was scoffed at by the political elite from both the Clinton and Bush Jr. administrations, turned out to be completely vindicated by the events of the next fifteen years. China's admission to the WTO, an incredibly corrupt organization in its own right, allowed a declared adversary to do to American industry what an ally, Japan, had done in a smaller way during the 1980s.

By 2020, we were reliant on China for medical and other supplies, during a pandemic that China itself created through its negligent (or worse) operation of a bioweapons lab in Wuhan. This reality was not lost on President Trump. In 2020, he remarked,

> It was only when [China] came into the World Trade Organization that they became a rocket ship because they took advantage. . . . How stupid were the people that stood here and allowed it to happen?

During the presidency of Jimmy Carter, the country was suffering from extreme inflation, a politically engineered energy crisis, and our great cities were decaying due to crime and economic divestment. The late 1970s was also the beginning of a terrible homeless crisis across many cities.

While President Carter was a decent man who was simply incapable of running the country, President Biden produced results that were worse, but unlike Carter, Biden resorted to a hitherto unknown campaign to imprison his principal political opponent and the allies of this opponent.

Many people who were willing to give Biden a chance in 2020 had become totally fed up with the decline in living standards and security before his single term in the White House was even half-way over. Adding to this was the worst border crisis in the history of the United States, arguably the worst in the world.

The aggregate effect of these crises led many who had been willing to give Biden a try, to feel a supreme sense of buyer's remorse. America wanted President Trump back. While "comedians" like the habitually unfunny and outwardly pathetic Jimmy Kimmel or the moribund and weird John Oliver continued to pretend that Sleepy Joe was doing a great job, everyone else knew better.

Even Democrats from blue cities in blue states began to shudder in horror at the amount of money being spent to house criminal illegal aliens in formerly beautiful hotels. While this was going on, basic public services were being cut like never before.

Most of these observations were articulated by Joe Rogan, a self-described progressive and former Democrat voter. On many occasions, Rogan explained that he had voted for Democrats in the past because as a child, his mother received welfare, and welfare programs tended to be more strongly associated with the Democrats. But as someone with a common-sense view of how the world ought to be run, Rogan became horrified at what Democrats did to California during Covid. As a result of the economically ruinous and anti-liberty politics of that state's governor, Gavin Newsom, Rogan made the decision to relocate his home and business to Texas, a Republican majority state.

When Biden's people got their hands on the levers of government, Rogan realized that many of the things he ran from in California were now realities within the White House. While the economy tanked and our adversaries mocked us, all we got were lectures about how women have penises, white lives do not matter, and January 6 was worse than 9/11 and Pearl Harbor combined. This was more than an assault on our economy and liberty, it was also an assault on common sense.

From the time of Euripides to that time you had a fun night at your local comedy club, laughter has always been a serious way to convey important information and to express well-developed opinions. Because of this, it was no surprise that it was the podcasting comedians who first sounded the alarm on a Biden administration that was built on a house of cards.

While Rogan became one of the most trusted and reassuring voices for millions of Americans, other legendary comedians with podcasts also sounded the national wake-up call that told the public it was more than okay to admit that Sleepy Joe Biden was a terrible leader. Names like Adam Carolla, Theo Von, and Tim Dillon became voices of comedic common sense that meticulously exposed the total lack of common sense that underpinned every policy of Sleepy Joe's White House.

While many of these comedians still do not consider themselves Republicans, Rogan and his comedic colleagues came to symbolize a coast-to-coast rebellion against the irrational, unworkable, and miserable policies of Biden.

The voters who embraced President Trump after hearing that they were not alone in feeling dejected by the national decay ushered in by Biden, can and should be called "The Rogan Republicans." These are people who may not have had any affinity to past Republican elected officials, but who realized that in the battle for common sense, the party of President Trump was the only clear choice over the party of increasingly unhinged rhetoric, policies, and enforcement mechanisms.

These Rogan Republicans provided therapeutic relief to those who felt that due to social pressures from the dying, fake, old media, they could not or should not express their longing for President Trump's return.

Rogan and other comedians with podcasts signaled to

Americans that it was not just logical to want President Trump back, it was cool too. President Trump was about to change pop culture yet again, in ways far more profound than ever before.

CHAPTER 10

Podcasting the Presidency

One of President Trump's greatest virtues is his refusal to refuse an interview. Whether on the tarmac of an airport after a rally, on the grounds of the White House, or in a studio owned by one of the networks that slanders him 24/7, President Trump is happy to talk to anyone in the media, anywhere, anytime.

President Eisenhower presided over the age in which television went from an obscure technology to a major part of every American household. President Reagan presided over a period where the personal computer became an increasingly visible part of work life. Likewise, President Trump presided over an age in which the podcast, in all of its many forms, became a more trusted source of news and views for the average American than the long-running programs on the networks or the related content on cable news channels.

The podcast is something that could have only been conceived in America. Anyone can start a podcast, and while some have the backing of major sponsors, most begin organically and grow as a result of grassroots popularity over time. Some podcasts are hosted by the green and curious while others are hosted by thought leaders and intellectuals. Some are hosted by hobbyists and specialists while others are hosted by keen observers of life and modern-day explorers. But the most successful podcasts have been and continue to be those hosted by comedians.

One of the first podcasts to gain a critical mass of listeners was the Adam Carolla Show. Carolla had been a staple of West Coast talk radio when his show was abruptly cancelled by the notoriously and increasingly fickle world of corporate radio. Without losing a step, Carolla obtained the necessary equipment to start podcasting from his home.

Unchained from the restrictions of both the FCC and corporate control, Carolla could go on rants that were neither curtailed by governmental censorship regulations nor limited by the time constraints inherent in commercial radio. Less than two years after the inception of Carolla's podcast, it had become the most downloaded internet-based show in history. Even in its first week, it was downloaded by nearly two million listeners. Something big was around the corner.

Months after Carolla started his podcast, fellow comedian Joe Rogan started his. Rogan's was even more informal and low budget. Over time, Rogan's podcast went from being a "shits and giggles" informal chat with fellow comedians and fellow martial artists, to the most popular podcast in the world. Ironically, both Rogan and his regular guest, Doug Stanhope, once hosted a version of cable's *The Man Show*, which was co-created and most famously co-hosted by Adam Carolla. Small worlds truly conquer big ones!

Today, podcasts are where the true conversations take place. The format has become invincible due to its immediacy, versatility, and honesty. The big budget world of legacy media simply cannot keep up. If not for the ability of large publicly traded companies to win licensing rights to major sporting events, it is difficult to say if the old networks would have survived into the 2020s. Even when they are watched, most younger people watch them via streaming apps.

President Trump is unique in that he represents timeless values while also cultivating futuristic innovation. He was the first person to achieve celebrity in the world of business *before* entering show business. Depending on when you came of age, you might remember President Trump more for telling Larry King and Charlie Rose about the New York property market, or you'll remember him better for roasting contestants on *The Apprentice*. But during the 2024 election cycle, a younger person might well think of Trump as the president who did more podcasts than every previous president combined.

These podcast appearances allowed the public to see a side of President Trump that previously was only known to those who spent time in his presence. The erudition with which the president spoke, whether talking about historic boxing matches and UFC matches, geopolitical strategy, or macroeconomics, made it abundantly clear that not only does President Trump have the memory of a wise elephant, but his rapid ability to poignantly and incisively analyze historic realities is second to none.

One viral and moving podcast moment came when comedian Theo Von recounted how he overcame an addiction to cocaine. Where some politicians would have scoffed and others would have pretended to be something they are not, President Trump displayed an authentic curiosity about addiction while expressing a sincere empathy for those who face such struggles.

The freewheeling podcast format allows for both in-depth conversations and discussions that float freely between multiple topics ranging from the sublime to the casual. This was a format tailor-made for a mind like that of President Trump's.

As a highly successful businessman, President Trump's unique insights into how the economy functions for real people in the real world sets him apart from career politicians who never functioned in the private sector. While legacy media sound bite interviews aim for short answers to hostile questions, most podcasts aim for elongated responses to authentic questions. It was on these podcasts that President Trump had the space to fully lay out his analysis of the many things wrong with Sleepy Joe's sleepy economy, while then laying out his highly specific solutions to making the economy function again.

Interspersed with this serious economic analysis were interesting responses to the pop and celebrity culture that President Trump had long been a part of. In a memorable podcast with the Nelk Boys, President Trump recounted golfing with O. J. Simpson, and offered his thoughts on Ice Spice, who at the time was in the first five minutes of her requisite fifteen minutes of fame.

As the election cycle moved forward, President Trump appeared on podcasts with an ever-younger demographic, most notably, a podcast interview with Kick steamer Adin Ross.

While President Trump was comfortable on the intellectual podcast of the engineer Lex Fridman, he was equally comfortable on the younger shows where IRL streamers and "edge lords" are the typical fare. President Trump credited his youngest son, Barron Trump, with recommending interviews on podcasts and streams featuring Gen Z hosts.

Between 2020 and 2024, young people began to feel the pinch of Bidenflation and the lack of business and job opportunities that resulted in one of the worst economies in modern history.

This was one of the matters I raised with the president at our lengthy meeting in 2023 at Mar-a-Lago. Young men are instinctively President Trump's core base. Consider the values and aspirations of young men in the 2020s. They have grown up admiring self-made men who go out on their own at a young age, blaze trails, and innovate in the fields of both technology and science as well as entertainment and other creative sectors. These young men value prosperity but also value a more authentic approach to life than prior generations, who were content to climb their way up company ladders, one cubicle at a time.

President Trump is emblematic of these values. He is someone who quickly made his own way in the world of business and adapted his approach to business as the world around him evolved. Had he decided to launch his famous show at a later date, *The Apprentice* could have easily been a video-based podcast that would have attracted the same high numbers of viewers that it did on NBC.

The only reason that in 2020, some young men found it difficult to express their natural inclinations to favor President Trump, was due to the relentless stereotypes of President Trump that extremely well-funded smear campaigns projected into the broader pop culture. To overcome this, I explained that both he and his surrogates would need to go directly to young men while cutting out the middlemen.

To accomplish this, President Trump needed to embrace the new world of new media, while I had to take the fight to young men across the country. I registered thousands of such men to vote in the process. Such a ground campaign helped to beat the Democrats at their own games involving strategic registration events and voter harvesting.

The aggregate result of these efforts showed the wider world what I already knew. Young men are not naturally progressive.

There is no logical reason that young men would adopt a progressive ideology that is opposed to male excellence, achievement, innovation, and success. The only explanation for the adoption of this ideology by *some* young men is external pressure. In order to survive in hostile environments, men, like creatures of the animal kingdom, will often adopt traits that are not natural to one's own reflexes, in order to preserve one's life.

By reaching out to young men in the places where they feel comfortable to engage in and listen to elongated conversations, President Trump had a timeless message for young men who had been simultaneously assaulted by the feminized, leftist education system, Hollywood, and anti-male Democrat politicians.

Put simply, the message was: You are not alone. You can be yourselves, and when the country has a *real* president back, you will be unleashed so that you can achieve every ounce of success you are willing to work for.

In sending this message, President Trump helped to shatter multiple vicious stereotypes that the legacy media had attempted to shackle him with. The most appalling lie of all is that President Trump has racist views. This could not be further from the truth. President Trump is someone who values and respects excellence in all people. As a businessman he worked with men of all backgrounds to see his creations come to life. Whether a new building, golf course, or entertainment program, President Trump's view is that greatness must be achieved and that anyone who achieves it is great.

His personal friendships with athletes, musicians, actors, and comedians over the decades is testament to the fact that President Trump recognizes talent across multiple industries and sectors.

While President Trump has more energy than your average middle linebacker, a new slanderous lie was invented about the president, following the decision of the Democrats to eject Joe Biden in favor of Kamala Harris. This new line of attack was that President Trump is "too old" to be the president. Nevermind that the exact same people spitting this rhetoric into existence had just weeks before insisted that not only was Sleepy Joe fit to hold office, but that his mental acumen was beyond reproach.

It was always advisable for the president to reach out directly to young men, as I made clear over a year before we saw the ritualistic humiliation of Sleepy Joe before the cackler.

Following the brief rise and prolonged fall of Kamala Harris, this strategy had an added bonus of demonstrating how President Trump actually was vastly more aware of the desires of young people than the younger but far less intelligent Harris.

President Trump proved that young people do not want a costume of familiarity, but instead want wisdom, intellectual curiosity, and a profoundly open mind when it comes to the issues they want addressed. Sure, Kamala Harris can shake her hips with Megan Thee Stallion and Beyonce so long as the check clears, but the age of familiar politics is over. The era of Bill Clinton winning votes by playing the saxophone on the *Arsenio Hall Show* is not even a memory for Gen Z.

Someone who is true to himself is much more valued among the young than someone who looks the part but has no substance. This is why President Trump was able to inspire so many young voters, and young men in particular.

A free concert at a Kamala Harris rally lasts a few hours. An economy that works for rather than against the interests of young people pays dividends for decades.

I cannot think of any political figure who could walk into a UFC event and receive more cheers than any of the fighters. Beyond this, President Trump is popular among the fighters because they recognize that he embodies many of the qualities of the great martial artists: discipline, an unshakable work ethic, respect for those who stand beside him, and a fierce drive to take down opponents.

President Trump was never far from the epicenter of pop culture. From his many movie and TV cameos to his memorable commercials to name drops in music, President Trump has always been a figure of great national affection.

The reason that many celebrities who had previously liked or even loved President Trump decided to turn against him in 2016 is because such people were acting in what they thought was their professional self-interest. Such people failed to understand that the movement President Trump was building was just as much about popular culture and popular sentiment as it was about the nuts and bolts of Washington, DC policy making.

In the 2024 campaign, millions of Americans rekindled their love of President Trump, not just because of his political leadership but because of his defining role in popular culture. This included many celebrities who returned to the "Trump train" when it finally dawned on them that President Trump was far cooler and more important to the turning tide of popular culture than your average star of the movie or music industries.

Just as President Trump hosted major concerts and cultural events for artists as diverse as Michael Jackson and Luciano Pavarotti in the 1990s and 2000s, so too has his second term begun with a galaxy of stars ranging from Snoop Dogg to Carrie Underwood.

The legacy media tried to destroy President Trump; instead he destroyed the old media and helped solidify the role of the new media in paving the way for a more honest America.

Chapter 11

The Greatest Mugshot of All Time

Some people think that democracy versus the lack thereof is what primarily distinguishes the politics of the Third World from that of the first. The facts tell a different story. The majority of Third World countries have elections and while many are rigged at the ballot box, many are not.

Does this mean that the Third World has free and fair politics? It most certainly does not. Far too often, when broadly fair elections result in the "wrong" choice, according to the *true power* behind the state, the electoral victors will be arrested on bogus corruption charges, political parties will be banned under the guise that they are "violent" or "extreme," and in other instances the candidate popular with the people but unpopular with the ruling elite will simply be killed. Sometimes this will be made to look like an accident and sometimes it will not.

After being suspiciously ousted from power in 2022, Pakistan's most popular modern Prime Minister, Imran Khan, was placed under arrest in 2023. In Burma/Myanmar, a country where the military runs the show, multiple politicians with varying democratic mandates have been in and out of prison for the last twenty years.

In 2011, sitting Filipino President Gloria Macapagal Arroyo was arrested. In Brazil, Peru, and Ecuador, the arrests and exile of major political leaders is commonplace.

There is therefore nothing unusual about the arrest or indictment of a major American political leader, except for the fact that unlike these Third World countries, the United States has a long history of civility and political normality compared to countries to whom few look for guidance in how to manage an honest and effective political system.

One of the reasons that the United States has never gone down the road of arrest and prosecuting political opponents is the First Amendment.

Our First Amendment does *not give* us the right to free speech. This was understood by the Founding Fathers as a right derived from God-given **natural law**. What the First Amendment does do, is **restrict the government** from making any law that would restrict our ability to speak, assemble, and worship freely.

Our First Amendment is globally unique. While some (but increasingly few) First World countries gift their citizens with the right to speak freely sometimes and on certain issues, the First Amendment is a dam against government intrusion into the expression of our thoughts, our remonstration of grievances, and our ability to worship God according to our beliefs rather than those of the ruling elites. This has allowed a political system to flourish whereby politicians can say anything without the fear of arbitrary arrest or incarceration, something that is highly prevalent not only in one-party dictatorships but also in the putative democracies that are scattered throughout the capitals of the Third World.

In addition to the First Amendment, the unspoken rule of American politics was one where political rivalries were left on the field. In the 1950s, conservative Republican Senator Barry Goldwater developed a close friendship with Senator John F. Kennedy. Their friendship was one that lasted until Kennedy's tragic assassination. Such friendships were common in politics and to some degree still are.

When President Johnson succeeded Kennedy following his demise, he introduced a style of brutal and crude politics that contrasted sharply with both the patrician Kennedy and the war hero gentleman that was President Eisenhower. Yet even under Johnson, it would have been unthinkable for any former President to be arrested

While President Andrew Jackson's opponents loathed his populism, there has never been a president in American history who was attacked more viciously and barbarously by his opponents than President Trump. The hitherto unthinkable mass censorship of a sitting president that occurred in the final weeks of President Trump's first term was a harbinger for what can only be called an open conspiracy against President Trump ever returning to the White House.

The Democrats and RINO opponents of President Trump wanted him silenced, forgotten, and kept far away from power. They sought for President Trump a Napoleonic exile. If anybody thinks this is normal, chances are that you do not possess the common decency of a normal American. Make no mistake, the Democrats and the RINOs went **full Third World,** and you never go **full** Third World.

While the second impeachment of President Trump in the

final week of his first term was a circus-like performative act that is perhaps most remembered for Senator Chuck Schumer accusing President Trump of causing an "erection," the Democrats and RINOs had much bigger plans for the future.

Whenever Democrats talk about a "national healing," you ought to hear what a wise consumer hears when a used car salesman offers you a lifetime warranty on that 1981 fully loaded Yugo. It's a pile of garbage.

If the Democrats wanted unity, they would have accorded President Trump the dignity commensurate with the highest political office in the world, rather than treat him *worse* than the human smugglers who are afforded every privilege of "human rights" for their crimes of bringing illegal aliens onto US soil.

Ironically, unlike some old guard Republicans, the Democrats were fully aware that a majority of Republican voters and a large number of Independents wanted President Trump to run in the 2024 election. His popularity remained not only intact, but many felt that he was owed his second term after witnessing all of the hanky-panky that occurred during the 2020 vote.

Just how could such momentum be stopped? Well, there are several ways. The Biden/Harris administration could have continued President Trump's successful economic policies and distracted people with prosperity. But that was never going to happen. The Democrats could have prepared to debate President Trump on his politics and record, but that was never in the cards. They could have held a genuine primary in the 2024 cycle rather than place a crown on the increasingly vacuous head of Sleepy Joe, but that wasn't part of the plan. Instead, they went down a dark, devious, and un-American route of throwing multiple bogus criminal charges at the man who was almost certain to run for president in 2024.

The first indictment against President Trump came in March

2023. The message the Democrats intended to send was crystal clear: "Do not run in 2024 because if you do, we will be unrelenting."

If anything, this tactic only made President Trump's supporters *more* invigorated. Now they had another reason to vote for President Trump a third time. It was no longer just about a return to the successful policies of the first Trump term, nor was it just about correcting the irregularities of 2020. Now it was about fighting against a system so corrupt that it stretched to all three branches of government, including the supposedly politically neutral judiciary.

If the Democrats couldn't scare President Trump into submission, they would do all they could to keep him off of the campaign trail and in the courtroom. While President Trump's Manhattan persecutors were wise enough (from their tactical position) not to take a mugshot or allow exculpatory cameras in the courtroom, this was not the case in Fulton County, Georgia.

By the time that August 24, 2023, rolled around, the news was out. After much speculation and innuendo, President Trump *would* in fact have a mugshot taken at the Fulton County Jail. That day, everyone's attention was turned to the helicopter shots of President Trump's motorcade driving to the jail. These words feel surreal to write, but that was how far our country had fallen. And then the world waited. Was it really going to happen? Could the Democrats and their allies in the Fulton County DA's office be that stupid? Will it look as cool as we were all hoping it would? By now, social media was flooded with AI-generated and photoshopped mugshots that were clearly fake. And then it happened.

The greatest mugshot of all time was released. It was the most viral image of all time up to that point, only to be surpassed by another viral image of President Trump the following year.

Since then, the mugshot has appeared on mugs, T-shirts, bumper stickers, posters, billboards, music videos, and memes. It was the photograph that made the world stand still. President Trump had done it again. His unique charisma, his star power, if you will, could not be dampened even by the most unjust thing to ever happen to any American politician.

The greatest mugshot of all time marked a key turning point in the election. From my experience registering voters and campaigning on the ground for President Trump, I was fully aware that all the public momentum was behind a re-election even before the mugshot. But after the mugshot, something palpable changed. Like a new season of *The Apprentice* combined with the opening of a new Trump property, all wrapped up in an inauguration party, President Trump was back at the front and center, not only of politics but of the culture.

As the kids say, Trump was the "OG" and he looked tough, strong, and bold in the picture seen around the world. Suddenly everyone wanted a piece of President Trump. If mugshots of Elvis Presley and Frank Sinatra were cool, with all due respect to two of the greatest entertainers of all time, this was cooler.

To this day, it is not easy to ascertain what the Democrats hoped to accomplish with this. One preposterous theory floated at the time was that the mugshot would galvanize the Republican base against President Trump's opponents in the GOP primaries, thus leading to a reality where an "easy to beat Trump" would fall to Joe Biden during the general election.

I knew that this was hogwash at the time and history validated my hypothesis. Others have suggested that the Democrats genuinely felt that the mugshot would make President Trump "unelectable" among the majority of *all* Americans, but even a cursory understanding of the realities on the ground would lead to a rational thinker quickly dismissing this notion.

I would suggest that in their hubris and their wickedness, DNC leaders felt that they actually stood a chance of removing President Trump from the campaign trail by forcing him to ping-pong between various courtrooms for the duration of 2024. Beyond this, it is my belief that the Democrats actually sought to imprison President Trump and hope that this would create a legal minefield between his prison cell and the White House door.

The Democrats proved to be the victims of their own political bubble. In their hive minds, they actually felt that the voting public was paying attention to the asinine details of these totally fake and frivolous legal matters. In reality, Americans were killed and destroyed by inflation. Mortgages were unattainable and unaffordable. The price of food was becoming so high that the land of plenty had become the land of hunger for millions of hardworking families.

Gas prices kept going up and Sleepy Joe had no plan to fix this other than plans that would force Americans to buy the expensive electric vehicles that a majority of Americans do not want. His other plan was to weaken national security by draining our strategic oil reserves in what should have been an impeachable offense.

The real America was in pain. They knew that the malice and ineptitude of the Biden/Harris administration was the source of this pain. Not being born yesterday, these real Americans knew that when President Trump was in the White House, life was more affordable, jobs were easier to secure, businesses were easier to open and expand, the stock market was healthier, retirement plans worked, and we were a nation that justifiably commanded respect.

It was at that time that I knew I must personally do something to preserve and revive our cherished First Amendment. This is why I have started a new group called 1A Warriors.

1A Warriors not only defends our freedom to speak and assemble, but also defends our civil liberties in the face of retribution from public and private organizations alike, as a "consequence" of our robust utilization of our God-given First Amendment.

No amount of paid sock puppet "influencers" could convince the public otherwise. What the public knew was that life was *much* better under President Trump and that his mugshot made him the coolest man on the planet. The Democrats had opened a Pandora's Box on themselves. They had made their opponent more popular than ever and more intrinsic to pop culture than ever. The OG was well on his way to beating the increasingly senile old president.

The greatest mugshot of all time also resulted in a thaw between President Trump and the X platform. While Elon Musk rectified the scandalous censorship of President Trump's Twitter account shortly after he acquired Twitter in late 2022, President Trump continued to post exclusively on Truth Social.

However, on the day that the mugshot was released, President Trump posted the image on X. This itself was the beginning of new great things to come in the following year.

President Donald Trump salutes while inspecting the troops during the sixtieth presidential inauguration in Emancipation Hall of the US Capitol on January 20, 2025, in Washington, DC. (Photo by Al Drago - Pool/Getty Images)

President Ronald Reagan (1911–2004) shakes hands with real estate developer Donald Trump in a reception line in the White House's Blue Room, Washington, DC, November 3, 1987. The reception was held for members of the Friends of Art and Preservation in Embassies Foundation. (Photo by White House Photo Office/PhotoQuest/Getty Images)

Donald Trump and Fred Trump attend a book release party to celebrate *Trump: The Art of the Deal* in the Trump Tower Atrium, New York City, December 12, 1987. (Photo by Sonia Moskowitz/Getty Images)

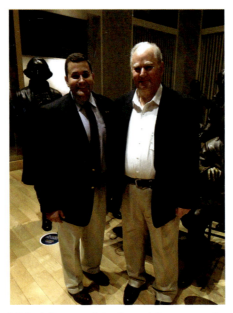

Nick Adams and Andrew Adams attending a convention at the National Constitution Center in Philadelphia, Pennsylvania, on September 15, 2017. (Photo courtesy of the author)

(Original Caption) Washington: Refusing to call himself the "front runner," Ronald Reagan opened the Washington phase of a likely 1980 bid for the GOP presidential nomination by meeting with a score of Republican senators. Here, he lunches with Sen. Barry Goldwater of Arizona. (Bettmann/Contributor/Getty Images)

President William McKinley making his "What a mighty power for good is a united nation" speech while addressing an audience in Memphis, Tennessee, circa 1901. (Photo by Hulton Archive/Getty Images)

Donald Trump, real estate mogul, entrepreneur, and billionaire, August 1987, New York City. (Photo by Joe McNally/Getty Images)

Donald Trump, Donald Trump, Jr., and Ivanka Trump during the *Celebrity Apprentice* live season finale on May 16, 2010, in New York City. (Photo by Bill Tompkins/Getty Images)

Democratic presidential nominee former Secretary of State Hillary Clinton walks off stage as Republican presidential nominee Donald Trump smiles after the third US presidential debate at the Thomas & Mack Center on October 19, 2016, in Las Vegas, Nevada. (Photo by Chip Somodevilla/Getty Images)

Former President Barack Obama and former Vice President Joe Biden congratulate President Donald Trump after he took the oath of office on the West Front of the US Capitol on January 20, 2017. (Photo by Chip Somodevilla/Getty Images)

President Donald Trump arrives to deliver the State of the Union address in the chamber of the US House of Representatives at the Capitol Building on February 5, 2019, in Washington, DC. (Photo by Doug Mills-Pool/Getty Images)

President Donald Trump and French President Emmanuel Macron stand as American Battle of Normandy veterans and family members look on during the main ceremony to mark the seventy-fifth anniversary of the World War II Allied D-Day invasion of Normandy at Normandy American Cemetery on June 6, 2019, near Colleville-Sur-Mer, France. (Photo by Sean Gallup/Getty Images)

President Donald Trump participates in the coin toss before the game between the Army Black Knights and the Navy Midshipmen at Lincoln Financial Field on December 14, 2019, in Philadelphia, Pennsylvania. (Photo by Elsa/Getty Images)

President Donald Trump is welcomed by Japanese Prime Minister Shinzo Abe as he arrives to play golf at Mobara Country Club on May 26, 2019, in Chiba, Japan. (Photo by Kimimasa Mayama - Pool/Getty Images)

A handout photo provided by Dong-A Ilbo of North Korean leader Kim Jong Un and President Donald Trump inside the demilitarized zone (DMZ) separating the South and North Korea on June 30, 2019, in Panmunjom, South Korea. (Handout photo by Dong-A Ilbo via Getty Images/Getty Images)

Nick Adams with President Donald Trump at his Mar-a-Lago office meeting to discuss election strategy for the 2024 presidential campaign, February 28, 2023. (Photo courtesy of the author)

Nick Adams with President Donald Trump at a campaign event in California, June 7, 2024. (Photo courtesy of the author)

Republican presidential candidate former President Donald Trump after being grazed by a bullet during a rally on July 13, 2024, in Butler, Pennsylvania. (Photo by Anna Moneymaker/Getty Images)

Republican presidential candidate former President Donald Trump is rushed offstage during a rally on July 13, 2024, in Butler, Pennsylvania. (Photo by Anna Moneymaker/Getty Images)

Former Republican presidential candidate Robert F. Kennedy Jr. and Republican presidential nominee, former President Donald Trump shake hands during a campaign rally at Desert Diamond Arena on August 23, 2024, in Glendale, Arizona. (Photo by Rebecca Noble/Getty Images)

Republican presidential nominee, former President Donald Trump holds a town hall campaign event with former Representative Tulsi Gabbard (I-HI) on August 29, 2024, in La Crosse, Wisconsin. (Photo by Scott Olson/Getty Images)

Republican presidential nominee former President Donald Trump attends a game between the NFL Pittsburgh Steelers and the New York Jets on October 20, 2024, in Latrobe, Pennsylvania. (Photo by Evan Vucci-Pool/Getty Images)

Republican presidential nominee former President Donald Trump holds a press conference from inside trash hauler at Green Bay Austin Straubel International Airport on October 30, 2024, in Green Bay, Wisconsin. (Photo by Chip Somodevilla/Getty Images)

Donald Trump is sworn into office by Supreme Court Chief Justice John Roberts as Melania Trump holds the Bible in the US Capitol Rotunda on January 20, 2025, in Washington, DC. Donald Trump takes office for his second term as the 47th president of the United States. (Photo by Julia Demaree Nikhinson - Pool/Getty Images)

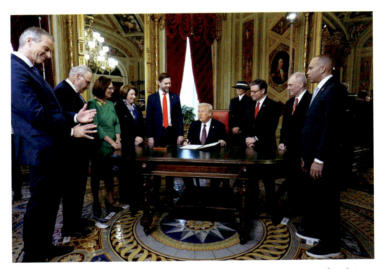

President Donald Trump takes part in a signing ceremony after his inauguration on January 20, 2025, in the President's Room at the US Capitol in Washington, DC. Also in attendance are: Senate Majority Leader Sen. John Thune (R-S.D.), Senate Minority Leader Sen. Chuck Schumer (D-N.Y.), Sen. Deb Fischer (R-NE), Sen. Amy Klobuchar (D-MN), Vice President J.D. Vance, Melania Trump, House Speaker Mike Johnson (R-LA), House Majority Leader Steve Scalise (R-LA) and House Minority Leader Hakeem Jeffries (D-NY). Photo by Melina Mara-Pool/Getty Images)

President Donald Trump reviews the troops in Emancipation Hall during his Inauguration ceremony at the US Capitol on January 20, 2025, in Washington, DC. (Photo by Greg Nash-Pool/Getty Images)

Second lady Usha Vance, Vice President J.D. Vance, President Donald Trump, and first lady Melania Trump wave as former President Joe Biden and former Vice President Kamala Harris depart the US Capitol on January 20, 2025, in Washington, DC. (Photo by Joe Raedle/Getty Images)

President Donald Trump addresses a joint session of Congress at the US Capitol on March 4, 2025, in Washington, DC. Vice President J.D. Vance and Speaker of the House Mike Johnson (R-LA) applaud behind him. (Photo by Win McNamee/Getty Images)

President Donald Trump speaks at the Justice Department March 14, 2025, in Washington, DC. (Photo by Andrew Harnik/Getty Images)

Former first lady Melania Trump joins Republican presidential nominee former President Donald Trump on stage after he officially accepted the Republican presidential nomination on the fourth day of the Republican National Convention at the Fiserv Forum on July 18, 2024, in Milwaukee, Wisconsin. (Photo by Andrew Harnik/Getty Images)

Chapter 12

Trump: A Man of Tradition

At the Republican National Convention of 1964, Barry Goldwater said,

> Now, my fellow Americans, the tide has been running against freedom. Our people have followed false prophets. We must, and we shall, return to proven ways—not because they are old, but because they are true.

Goldwater was referring to what he correctly identified as a political mood that, with something of a break during the peaceful and prosperous Eisenhower years, had been turning steadily towards collectivism rather than individualism ever since the conception of FDR's New Deal.

The unapologetically anti-communist Senator from Arizona helped to spark America's post-war conservative revolution, one that would not be fully realized at an executive level until 1980, when one of Goldwater's most visible surrogates became president himself. This man was President Ronald Reagan, a man whose victory in the 1966 California gubernatorial election was partly due to the political fame Reagan achieved campaigning for Goldwater.

President Reagan's two terms helped to solidify a new conservative consensus that would take the Republican party into the twenty-first century. However, much of this consensus was shattered after 9/11.

The administration of George W. Bush was eager to frame warfare in terms of liberationist ideology, failing to heed the following warning given by the Cold Warrior Goldwater:

> Now I know this freedom is not the fruit of every soil. I know that our own freedom was achieved through centuries, by unremitting efforts of brave and wise men. And, I know that the road to freedom is a long and a challenging road. And I know also that some men may walk away from it, that some men resist challenge, accepting the false security of governmental paternalism.

These words echo those of James Madison, who said the following about attempts to apply the letter and spirit of the US Constitution to those in foreign lands:

> Our Constitution was made only for a moral and religious People. It is wholly inadequate to the government of any other.

By the early 2000s, it seemed that the Republican party had forgotten this message. Warfare is costly in terms of both blood and treasure, and the George W. Bush administration was willing to sacrifice both in the name of democratizing countries that were and remain woefully ill equipped to handle the responsibility of constitutionally derived representative government.

Domestically, the big spending and the Patriot Act's blowtorch approach to constitutional liberty made Bush and Cheney look and feel like a significant departure from Reaganism. If the 1980 election was won with a single phrase, it could be attributed to President Reagan affirming that "In this present crisis, government is not the solution to our problem. Government is the problem."

The geopolitical experiments of the Bush years were comprehensively rejected by voters who were willing to take a chance on a hitherto unknown community organizer from Chicago who had not even served a full term in the Senate when he beat Hillary Clinton to become the Democratic presidential nominee in the 2008 election cycle.

Like Reagan, whose rise to *political* fame was based on the speeches he made for Goldwater, particularly a lengthy speech that was televised, so too was Obama's rise to political fame based on his 2004 speech made at the Democratic National Convention. Barack Obama's rhetoric was one that was all about looking to the future with the aim to reshape it. Because this futuristic message was cloaked in the optimism that Obama was able to deliver with such charisma, Americans literally saw Obama as an exponent of "hope" and "change."

The messages of "hope" and "change" are in fact uniquely American when presented in the political arena. In Europe, there exists a constant tension between the future and past. For European politics, the past carries with it the symptoms of feudalism to which few would want to return. But it is also true that in Europe the future has always represented something even worse: the gangsterism and destructive power of communism.

As a result, most Europeans have thrown up their hands and in so doing, they have consigned their political future to be one of technocratic tyranny whose only promise is to avoid both a return to neo-feudalism and full-on Stalinism. If this sounds depressing, it is because it is. Be grateful you do not live in Europe. While my birth nation of Australia is separated from Europe by two oceans, much of this political malaise has crept into the politics of the land down under.

But in the United States, the future is a place where new inventions become everyday items we cannot live without. It is the place where the sky's the limit. Americans walked on the moon and will someday conquer Mars because Americans aren't afraid of the future, they are confident that they will shape it and own it.

This is why Barack Obama was able to win. I said at the time that the fault among conservatives for losing two elections to Obama was due to our inability to offer a coherent future-looking alternative to the articulate Democrat.

I knew in 2008 that while Obama was good at selling hope, he would not be able to deliver. His view of society was of one defined not by shared achievements or even a shared past. It was one defined by an obsession with racial division where the blame squarely fell on the shoulders of the white, male, right-leaning men who Obama's White House imagined were all racists, even though the truth could not be more different.

Obama's initial victory came in an era when the social media ecosystem remained a space for the young. The older folks and the middle-aged remained reliant on the mainstream media for the daily dose of "information." This allowed Obama to sell very different messages to different demographics without any worry of cross talk.

In the first years of the Obama administration, there was a very real danger that the Occupy Wall Street movement would topple any attempts to create an economically centrist administration. Being keenly aware of this, the Obama administration moved to shift the narrative among the young from one of meat and potatoes economic grievance to the more obscure and often entirely fictional matters of racial and sexual grievance. The very European notion of identity politics was being successfully applied to American politics absent of any concrete political undertones.

What is meant by "absent of any concrete political undertones"? The racial politics of the 1960s had a very specific origin. There were those on the one hand who were in favor of preserving the Jim Crow laws of some Southern states and there were those on the other hand who wished to replace the Jim Crow laws with new federal Civil Rights legislation. There were also those who favored a fully libertarian approach to the matter, but their day would not come for some decades.

In other words, the racial politics of the 1960s was a form of identity politics that had to do with specific legislation in specific places at a specific time. Once the Supreme Court upheld the Civil Rights Act of 1964 with virtually all provisions intact, America's modern flirtation with identity politics faded away.

This contrasts sharply with the invention of a new identity politics that was conceived by those in the Obama administration who were losing sleep over Occupy Wall Street and its wide implications. The identity politics of the Obama era was much like Orwell's characterization of totalitarian states' approach to war: it was not intended to be resolved, it was intended to be endless.

Because of this, we saw a form of identity politics emerge in the United States that would have been familiar to much of Europe, and indeed, to much of the Third World. This was the identity politics which extolled the radicalism of those who were told "the American dream is not for you, but the soft-socialist Democrat version of America *is* for you."

This had devastating consequences to the idealism of Reaganite conservatism. Yet, the GOP seemed to have no plans to oppose Obamaism other than to offer Obamaism that drove the speed limit.

In the 2008 election, there was a famous incident during a live town hall event where Republican presidential nominee Senator John McCain was confronted with a voter who said that she did not trust Barack Obama because he is an "Arab." McCain grabbed the microphone from the concerned voter, and in a somewhat scolding tone said that Obama is a decent American with whom he merely has some policy disagreements.

The mainstream media praised McCain for putting this concerned voter "in her place." That was the moment McCain lost. While I agree with McCain that Obama is an American rather than an Arab, this does not strike at the essence of the concerned voter's question.

Had I been prepping McCain for such a question, I would have advised him to say the following. "While Senator Obama is an American man from an American family who is running in an American election, I share your worry that his politics represent a significant departure from the America we all know and love. This is not because of his middle name and certainly not because of the color of his skin. It is because the change of which he speaks is a step backwards. It is the politics of personal grievance rather than the politics of unshakable liberty. It is the politics of activism rather than the politics of pragmatism. It is the politics of divide and conquer, rather than that of Manifest Destiny. A vote for me is a vote to bring America back to its days of glory, to be better than we have ever been. This is the America I want for our children and grandchildren."

Had McCain said that, he may have won. But that was not John McCain and that was not the GOP of 2008.

While the GOP of Washington, DC was increasingly moribund in 2008, a new movement among the grassroots GOP was growing. The Tea Party Movement was the right's answer to Occupy Wall Street. While Occupy Wall Street protested against corporate greed, the Tea Party protested government overreach. Each movement was a reaction against the fiscal excesses of the Bush/Cheney administration.

What happened next played into the hands of Obama and his crowd. The Tea Party was unfairly characterized as a backward-looking movement filled with "white racists," while Obama supporters began framing the future as one in which racial, ethnic, and most perplexingly, sexual minorities would rule the roost.

Towards the end of Obama's second term, even he began to realize that the political monster he created was getting out of control. At first this seemed not to bother the Democrats. As Hillary Clinton was the presumptive Democrat nominee for 2016, even before she entered the race, a plan was in place to run her as the "continuity Obama."

They did not count on Donald J. Trump changing politics forever. President Trump totally shattered the future/past confrontational politics that existed between Obama's identitarians and the Tea Party.

President Trump promised to Make America Great Again, a direct appeal to those who wanted to step back from the brink of an identitarian meltdown and return to a time when America, looked, sounded, felt, and indeed was a place of comfortable familiarity, of traditional liberties, and of families and individuals who did not need to belong to a tribe or sect in order to feel validated.

President Trump's conception of Americanism can be summed up best in his own words that were offered to a crowd of supporters who gathered before Mount Rushmore on the 4th of July, 2020:

> We gather tonight to herald the most important day in the history of nations: July 4th, 1776. At those words, every American heart should swell with pride. Every American family should cheer with delight. And every American patriot should be filled with joy, because each of you lives in the most magnificent country in the history of the world, and it will soon be greater than ever before.

He added,

> It was all made possible by the courage of 56 patriots who gathered in Philadelphia 244 years ago and signed the Declaration of Independence. They enshrined a divine truth that changed the world forever when they said: "… all men are created equal."
>
> These immortal words set in motion the unstoppable march of freedom. Our Founders boldly declared that we are all endowed with the same divine rights — given [to] us by our Creator in Heaven. And that which God has given us, we will allow no one, ever, to take away — ever.
>
> Seventeen seventy-six represented the culmination of thousands of years of western civilization and the triumph not only of spirit, but of wisdom, philosophy, and reason.

No president of any party has delivered such a powerful encapsulation of what it means to be an American. Even if they could, they would have stopped there, but not President Trump.

President Trump is a realist who is completely unafraid to tackle a crisis at its inception. The year 2020 was, in hindsight, the year that the Obama coalition of "groups with grievances" exploded into overt violence. President Trump addressed this head on during his speech:

> And yet, as we meet here tonight, there is a growing danger that threatens every blessing our ancestors fought so hard for, struggled, they bled to secure.
>
> Our nation is witnessing a merciless campaign to wipe out our history, defame our heroes, erase our values, and indoctrinate our children.
>
> Angry mobs are trying to tear down statues of our Founders, deface our most sacred memorials, and unleash a wave of violent crime in our cities. Many of these people have no idea why they are doing this, but some know exactly what they are doing. They think the American people are weak and soft and submissive. But no, the American people are strong and proud, and they will not allow our country, and all of its values, history, and culture, to be taken from them.
>
> One of their political weapons is "Cancel Culture"—driving people from their jobs, shaming dissenters, and demanding total submission from anyone who disagrees. This is the very definition of totalitarianism, and it is completely alien to our culture and our values, and it has absolutely no place in the United States of America. This attack on our liberty, our magnificent liberty, must

be stopped, and it will be stopped very quickly. We will expose this dangerous movement, protect our nation's children, end this radical assault, and preserve our beloved American way of life.

In our schools, our newsrooms, even our corporate boardrooms, there is a new far-left fascism that demands absolute allegiance. If you do not speak its language, perform its rituals, recite its mantras, and follow its commandments, then you will be censored, banished, blacklisted, persecuted, and punished. It's not going to happen to us.

Make no mistake: This left-wing cultural revolution is designed to overthrow the American Revolution. In so doing, they would destroy the very civilization that rescued billions from poverty, disease, violence, and hunger, and that lifted humanity to new heights of achievement, discovery, and progress.

To make this possible, they are determined to tear down every statue, symbol, and memory of our national heritage.

President Trump further said,

The violent mayhem we have seen in the streets of cities that are run by liberal Democrats, in every case, is the predictable result of years of extreme indoctrination and bias in education, journalism, and other cultural institutions.

Against every law of society and nature, our children are taught in school to hate their own country, and to believe that the men and women who built it were not heroes, but that were villains. The radical view of American history is a web of lies—all perspective is removed, every virtue is obscured, every motive is twisted, every fact is distorted, and every flaw is magnified until the history is purged and the record is disfigured beyond all recognition.

This movement is openly attacking the legacies of every person on Mount Rushmore. They defile the memory of Washington, Jefferson, Lincoln, and Roosevelt. Today, we will set history and history's record straight.

In this speech, President Trump *saved* America from the fate of countries torn apart by sectarian violence. There was a real danger that the riotous plague that destroyed many Democrat-run cities in 2020 would eventually spread nationwide. We were not far away from being torn asunder in the way that Yugoslavia was in the 1990s.

President Trump identified the logical conclusion of the behavior of the monsters that Barack Obama cynically created in order to suppress what was ultimately a peaceful Occupy Wall Street movement. In its place were radical anti-American mobs who sought to bring down America and replace it with a tyrannical regime where socialism would replace freedom and where racial struggle sessions would replace our Bill of Rights.

Had the 2020 election been free and fair, President Trump would have solved these problems in the first months of 2021. Instead, the Biden/Harris administration normalized this radicalism. The violence of 2020 became the executive orders of 2021.

And then something happened. The American spirit of which President Trump spoke began to rise up. The spirit of 1776 began to extinguish the flames of a would-be Bolshevist 1917. People across the country saw the devastating results of an administration whose ruinous economy was only matched by its contempt for traditional American values.

But revolutions born of violence always end up eating their own. The Democrats found it increasingly difficult for their poster boy of racial and sexual grievance to be a senile rich white man who just a few years earlier had pretended to be a social moderate.

It was during this time that I rallied young men to believe in themselves and in America. They were hungry for a messenger who would deliver them the good news that masculine traits are virtuous and masculine social roles are the foundation on which society is built. It was also during this time that many women began to rebel against the Biden/Harris "values" that led to men dangling their penis and testicles before young girls in school locker rooms. This too is the legacy of Obama's "grievance groups."

Then we found out that Black Lives Matter was a giant fraud. Its leaders lived large, buying California mansions while preaching Marxist revolutionary ideology to the befuddled masses. We also grew more confident in saying that the lives of all Americans matter and this includes white men who are *not* named Biden—the only white family offered protection by the Democrats.

In other words, the nation got to experience firsthand that every word spoken by President Trump at Mount Rushmore was true and everything that his opponents had said was false.

The German philosopher Arthur Schopenhauer is often attributed with the expression, "All truth passes through three stages: first, it is ridiculed; second, it is violently opposed; and third, it is accepted as self-evident."

One could easily apply this maxim to that of President Trump. First his ideas are called ridiculous, then they are called dangerous, and then they are accepted as the only logical solutions to problems that others allowed to spiral out of control.

President Trump's 2024 election was an indication of his

vindication. Making America Great Again means many things. This includes making America sane, safe, and normal again.

The surging support for President Trump in the lead-up to his comeback victory was a sign that people yearn for the normal in place of the insane. They seek prosperity in the face of extreme inflation. They seek safety from the tyranny of the mob. They want a government that protects their life, liberty, and property rather than one that funds its destruction.

President Trump's vindication was a moment of national salvation and rebirth. It was a return to the traditions that made America great, but it was also about much more. It was about looking to the future in a real sense. The 1960s had transistors and moonshots but the Trump future was about to have even more.

Chapter 13

Trump: A Man of the Future

In both rhetoric and record, President Trump has done more than any political leader in generations to reconnect the country with its traditions. But this is only half the story. President Trump is a man of the future, a man who refuses to rest on successes of the past, but instead, holds those around him to similarly high standards to which he holds himself.

In the previous chapter, I discussed how only in the United States can past and future coexist harmoniously in the political realm. Where in other countries, these things are at odds on a deeply conceptual level, in the United States, anything is possible. In order to grasp President Trump's visionary and innovative approach, one should first consider what he was most renowned for before entering the political arena—his properties.

When Trump Tower opened in 1983, it was Manhattan's most architecturally daring and sophisticated structure that had been erected in over a decade. The 1970s was a difficult period for New York City and even in the early 1980s, few New Yorkers were imagining how their city could be revived.

Trump Tower's opening was a shot of adrenaline in the arm of a city that never slept easy, in a period where crime, decay, and arson were regular features that blighted the world's most famous skyline.

But 1983 was an inflection point, and with Trump Tower, a bold statement was made to the country and the world, New York City was back, and it was going to be taking residents and tourists on a nostalgia trip. The city now had a building that boldly declared a new future.

In the early eighties, most new construction in New York continued to be designed in the prevailing architectural school of the mid-twentieth century, the new international style. This architectural movement stressed clean angular lines and sparse ornamentation. Trump Tower cast this prevailing orthodoxy to the wind and instead exuded a warmer, more comforting, and more unique design. The exterior is dominated by a series of inverted pyramids that appear to defy gravity. This makes a bold statement. It is one that evokes scientific innovation to suggest power and strength to the passerby.

Once inside, the grand atrium invites visitors to look upwards and stand in awe of the great possibilities inherent in this bold architectural statement. At a time when interiors were black, white, and gray, the elegant stone and flowing fountains of Trump Tower felt like a place where the modern American would feel welcome.

President Trump built a structure fit for the future. The proof of this accomplishment lies in the fact that decades later, Trump Tower still feels brand new. The same spirit of limitless optimism that underscored the building's erection, continues to delight men and women from around the world who come to visit a monument to one man's vision of a New York City that can be more than it ever was before.

While President Trump's portfolios of skyscrapers continued to grow, in the 1990s, he set his sights not upwards but to the horizon. For President Trump golf is not a hobby, it is a competitive sport in which he has achieved unique excellence. I truly believe that if he went into golf as a professional, he would today be in the record books alongside the likes of Jack Nicklaus, Arnold Palmer, and Tiger Woods.

Prior to 1999, President Trump had played on the world's most prestigious golf courses, but as a man of action, he did not sit around and wait for someone else to build the course of his dreams. He decided to do it himself.

When the Trump International Golf Club opened in Palm Beach in November 1999, it was widely praised by athletes and industry leaders alike. Its ninth hole continues to be described as the most beautiful in the world. Not only did President Trump build a functional and competitive course, but he built one with a pristine beauty that can be appreciated even by someone who has never held a nine iron in his life.

President Trump's pre-politics innovation was not limited to his properties. In creating the most successful reality show of all time, President Trump created something unique in the world of twenty-first-century entertainment. *The Apprentice* did what no other major reality show aspired to do. It not only entertained, but it educated. In a country where anything is possible, President Trump gave millions of viewers a masterclass on entrepreneurialism and business. The show also gave millions of Americans a behind-the-scenes look at how the Trump business empire was run. We all got to know his family, so much so that they became America's honorary First Family even before they assumed this role in the formal sense.

The Apprentice taught many people the hard lessons that are needed to succeed in the fast-paced world of New York business. But even more, it reaffirmed that if you persevere, improve yourself constantly, never give up, and exude confidence, you will succeed.

President Trump's show was something that no network executive could have dreamt up. It was the kind of show that could only be produced through authenticity. The man seen on the show is the real Donald Trump. A man who is wise and detail-orientated but not at the expense of missing out on the big picture.

At a time when many reality TV shows were accurately described as being "fake," *The Apprentice* is remembered as a show that produced well-known figures who went on to major successful ventures across multiple sectors. The show was a Prime Time MBA.

When President Trump moved into the White House, Arnold Schwarzenegger attempted to step into the void. This version of *The Apprentice* was quickly cancelled. It turns out that you cannot *act* like a world class businessman and innovator, you have to be one.

President Trump reimagined New York City and as a result he changed the Manhattan skyline forever. President Trump reimagined the modern golf course and as a result, he elevated course quality for the pros while bringing the sport ever closer to the public.

In creating one of the most successful television shows of all time, President Trump rewrote the rules of reality TV and gave all Americans the insights of how major corporate boardrooms function behind closed doors.

All of this represents innovation across a wide variety of sectors including real estate, architecture, hospitality, entertainment, sports, landscaping, corporate governance, and education.

When running for president, Donald Trump leveraged technology more effectively than anyone before or since. This too should rightly be seen as a unique innovation that changed political communications strategies forever.

During his first term, President Trump turbocharged innovation. The racial and sexual obsessions of the Obama era gave way to an era where Americans were unleashed to do what they do best—innovate, invent, and excel in the world of both small and large scale business.

President Trump's creation of the US Space Force represented the most significant achievement in the annals of aerospace since the creation of NASA under President Eisenhower.

President Trump's second term is certain to be remembered as the most pro-technology of any presidential administration. While Sleepy Joe attempted to strangle the burgeoning US crypto sector with frivolous lawsuits and regulations designed to push crypto offshore, President Trump has pledged to make the United States the global leader in cryptocurrency.

On July 27, 2024, President Trump became the first American leader to ever address such a conference. While many of the so-called "crypto bros" in the audience cared little for electoral politics, the Biden/Harris attacks on the crypto industry proved to be a rude awakening for many.

President Trump's young audience uproariously applauded throughout his speech. Finally, they had a champion in Washington who understood their needs, encouraged their ambitions and promised to be an ally rather than a hindrance. By appointing David Sacks to an executive role in overseeing both crypto and Artificial Intelligence (AI), President Trump has assured that the future of American technology and cryptofinance is in the hands of someone from the world of business. Prior to this, the country's AI tsar was none other than Kamala Harris, a woman who clearly doesn't know the difference between BTC and a BLT.

Thousands of years later, we still admire that mathematical and scientific genius of the Ancient Greeks while marvelling equally at the architectural and engineering genius of the Ancient Romans. Modern Americans have likewise written our names in the stars. The age of Eisenhower and Kennedy was the Space Age. Not only did we go where no men had gone before, but our national investment in aerospace resulted in the greatest revolution in consumer electronics that the world had hitherto experienced.

The age of Reagan was the age when the personal computer took on its modern form. Companies like Apple and Microsoft thrived during Reagan's digital revolution. Knowing the extent of President Trump's commitment to technology, it is safe to venture that the Age of Trump may well be remembered as the age of consolidated and practical artificial intelligence.

The burdens of paperwork, research, and revelation that once slowed innovation have been lifted. We have yet to see the full extent of how the AI revolution will free the creative spirit for ever greater achievements, but I have no doubt that it will. Because of President Trump, the language of AI remains American English.

The age of Trump will also be a new golden era in the age of space exploration. The Apollo Program was the birth of our modern quest to conquer our galaxy, while the Space Shuttle Program defined the American renaissance of the Reagan era. Under George W. Bush and Barack Obama, our space program slowly died. Its salvation did not come from the crusted over halls of government but from a dynamic private sector.

The leading figure in this revitalization of our space program was and remains Elon Musk. His company SpaceX is a global pioneer in the once mythical field of reusable rockets. Like Trump, Musk has excelled at starting companies that refuse to be bound by the standards and expectations of the past. Also like Trump, Musk has taken failing companies and turned them into productive and profitable powerhouses.

SpaceX's satellite internet system, Starlink, has already revolutionized the internet. By allowing Americans to literally cut the cord, Starlink has connected Americans to a world of possibilities thanks to technology developed in the pursuit of Musk's ultimate goal—the human colonization of Mars.

During the Biden/Harris administration, Musk's success was a phenomenon that came to be despite multiple attempts by the White House to destroy his many companies. A cesspool of lawsuits, regulatory actions, and open threats risked destroying our national potential to achieve greatness across multiple high-tech fields.

The dynamics under President Trump could not be more different. Respecting a fellow genius, President Trump and Elon Musk work as partners to help government get out of the way of the great American mind and the great American company. It is still somewhat bemusing to hear leftists scoff at Musk's voluntary contributions to reduce government waste and overreach as part of President Trump's Department of Government Efficiency (DOGE). These same leftists have cheered on the supine role of billionaire George Soros in far-left politics.

And yet, Soros has contributed zero to American innovation, invention, and enterprise. He has never built a rocket, nor has he built a car. Soros never created the world's first affordable and user-friendly satellite internet service. He never drilled tunnels below the Nevada desert in what promises to be a revolution in personal transportation. Soros never developed battery systems that allow

American homeowners to live off the grid while powering their homes with solar energy.

All of these innovations are those of Musk, not Soros. The left has no problem with wealth, after all. But they do have a problem with meritocratic wealth creation. They likewise have no problem with billionaires, so long as the billionaire in question is a parasitic leftist rather than a common-sense innovator who used logic to determine that the only leader fit to take America into a *new* golden age is President Trump.

From Trump Tower to the White House and from Mar-a-Lago to Mars. President Trump's golden age is already one where the sky is the limit and where innovation knows no bounds.

America is back doing what she does best—leading the world in all that is new. The future will be American because the present is being guided by world class innovator-in-chief, Donald J. Trump.

Chapter 14

Generation T

Some leaders barely influence policy in any meaningful or long-lasting way, but others shape the mindsets of entire generations. Consider several modern American presidents and their impact on generational ethos. President Franklin D. Roosevelt changed the mindset of those who came of age under his lengthy time in the White House.

Because of FDR, millions of Americans began to see the federal government as a national custodian of personal and family social security. The New Deal generation saw the government programs launched by FDR as a sacrosanct part of the fabric of America.

Those who came of age under FDR tended to be too young to remember the strident and often bipartisan congressional and judicial opposition to his wide-reaching expansion of the federal government's role in the daily and economic lives of families and business owners, but instead tended to reflect positively on the changes his administrations instigated.

Perhaps even more than his leadership during the Second World War, it was the New Deal that transformed the way both veterans and their wives thought of society. This demonstrates that right or wrong, history-changing presidencies impact our sociology and culture as much as they impact what subsequent politicians say and do during election cycles.

While President Kennedy represented a proudly optimistic and patriotic sense of duty that influenced popular culture, his tragically brief time in office is often remembered as a contrast to what came next.

President Johnson's presidency shaped society due to the fact he was *not* a Kennedy. The era of Johnson is remembered as a diametric contrast to that of JFK. Optimism was replaced by cynicism. Honesty replaced by subterfuge. Poetic words about peace replaced by the prosaic realities of the least popular war in American history.

Although some leftist historians praise Johnson's wide reaching, socially interventionist legislative program, such apologias cannot change generational memories of Johnson any more than conservative critiques of FDR did anything to change the views of those who grew up under FDR.

The entire 1970s represents an era in which three presidents did little to leave lasting positive change on the psyches of the generation that grew up under Nixon, Ford, and Carter. While President Nixon was among the most personally intelligent of all our modern leaders, Watergate prohibited any of his positive achievements from shaping the consciousness of the "Nixon generation." The short presidency of Ford and the flawed presidency of Carter only reinforced the idea that the age of a highly influential president might be over for good, so far as the children of the 1970s were concerned.

But then came President Reagan. Not only did the Gipper prove that it was very much possible for a president to instigate generational change, but President Reagan had a greater generational impact than any leader since FDR, at the time. President Reagan challenged many of the post-New Deal orthodoxies whose sheen had worn very thin by the time he was elected. In doing so, he changed the center-left ideals that sprung up since the end of the New Deal.

While the era of President Eisenhower rolled back much of the radicalism of the New Deal era due to the calming social implications of an incredibly strong economy that helped to buttress and expand the middle class, he did not offer a clearly articulated vision of a post-New Deal America. This was partly intentional. Many of the men he led during the Second World War continued to see the New Deal era as one that was overwhelmingly positive from the standpoint of government's relationship to the citizen.

President Reagan's era was one where suburbia ceased being the target of jokes told by hippy comedians and one where highly driven young people no longer needed to merely whisper that they wanted to work hard so that they could buy a nice suburban home with at least two cars in the garage. President Reagan reacquainted the country with its middle-class foundations. The Vietnam era extolled the urban and the urbane, even as the 1970s saw many great cities fall into states of decline.

In this sense, President Reagan restored not only a strong economy that harkened back to the Eisenhower era, but more than even Ike himself, Reagan's generation felt that the archetypal setting of the American Dream was one to be extolled loudly while this dream would be defended against from all those who might diminish it. This is why President George H. W. Bush won in 1988. Bush was vastly less charismatic than Reagan and significantly less committed to Reagan's ideals of cutting the size and scope of government. However, when compared to his electoral opponent, Governor Michael Dukakis, Bush was seen as a capable custodian for the Reagan generation while Dukakis was seen as a throwback to the era that produced Jimmy Carter, urban decay, inflation, and a pop culture that mocked middle class values.

This is the power of a generation-shaping politician. First, his less able successors are forced to present themselves as individuals capable of managing the legacy of their predecessor and then something else happens—opponents are forced to shift the way they present their own politics.

In many ways, Arkansas Governor Bill Clinton was the least qualified Democrat who ran in the primary during the 1992 election cycle, but he had a secret weapon. President Clinton and his wife (a former Republican), realized that challenging the Reagan revolution would lose votes among Generation Reagan, those who came of age during a time when Reaganite values became the mainstream values of America's middle class.

As a result, Clinton toned down the leftist economic rhetoric of his predecessors and inaugurated an era in which image became more important than substance. This helped him to win in 1992, but it was something very different that created "Generation Clinton." While a less consequential leader (by far) than FDR or Reagan, the Clinton Generation was shaped not by any of the policies or rhetoric that came out of the Clinton White House, but by its most infamous scandal. While Watergate did not produce a generation of kids who aspired to break into the offices of their political opponents looking for dirt, President Clinton's scandal did shape future generations.

While the sexual revolution is typically considered a product of the 1960s, Clinton effectively "legalized" the sexual revolution. This is to say that prior to Clinton, the relaxed sexual standards of the 1960s were seen as something that was a "hobby" of the young that they would either grow out of or at least stop talking about once they reached a certain age.

Suddenly, adultery, lying about adultery, and vivid descriptions of oral sex and anal penetration with cigars went from the subject matter that was hidden in the back corner of video stores in the Reagan era, to something that was fodder for the nightly news and the dinner table. The impact of this cannot be overstated. Clinton's "legalization" (e.g., legitimization) and elevation of the sexual revolution ended up creating a vastly more cynical generation of Americans than those who grew up with the wholesome and inspired optimism of Reagan.

President George W. Bush's attitude to foreign policy in the aftermath of the tragic events of 9/11 only served to reinforce this cynicism. After campaigning against "nation building," Bush not only broke his promise to the Republicans who admire the common-sense patriotism of Senator Robert Taft, but he drove a generational wedge between the GOP and the young people of America, one that ran the risk of being irreparable until President Trump declared his candidacy in 2015.

While a very different character than Bush or Clinton, President Obama's cynical manipulation of racial and sexual politics represented a continued chapter in the growing cynicism of a once optimistic country that began under Clinton. This left many Americans, including those who were not particularly political, asking themselves if we could ever recover our optimism?

The answer came from a man whose life, words and deeds exudes optimism. The answer "Yes," came from President Trump.

While the legacy media often focuses solely on the views and grievances of past generations, the new media allows the wider public to get inside the heads of those coming of age in real time. Because of this, the verdict on President Trump is already clear.

Young people love President Trump. Even those who are apolitical love the things he stands for.

What then are the values of Generation T, the young people who are coming of age under Trump's presidency—the people who, when they grow up, will be the leaders of tomorrow's businesses, cultural institutions, and political parties?

The members of Generation T not only think that anything is possible to do, they think that anything is possible to invent. Generation T aspires to become successful, self-made men and women. They see a problem and are already imagining a solution.

These are the people I have interacted with, inspired, and registered to vote across the country. These people, while optimistic, are not blindly optimistic. They are well aware that previous leaders have taken away the quick and "easy" roots to success that their parents enjoyed. But unlike the cynical generations that grew up under Clinton, Bush, and Obama, Generation T is filled with the fire that tells itself that greatness is possible if you fight like hell to achieve it and spend every day learning how to make such greatness possible.

Generation T is comprised of strong men made by the hard times created by President Trump's predecessors. Generation T will consequently be the generation to secure a permanently better America, having been unleashed by the hitherto unknown prosperity that President Trump's second term represents.

Unlike the New Deal generation, Generation T does not expect the government to help them along the way, and unlike Generation Reagan, Generation T does not expect the age-old institutions of the private sector to behave as they once did.

Generation T members are akin to the pioneers of nineteenth century America. These young people are the pioneers of America's New Golden Age. They will conquer Mars and conquer the culture. They will use common sense to make America fun again. They will use humor to disarm that shrieking protestations of the more cautious and cynical failures of previous generations.

The children of Trump have more in common with the spirit of 1776 than any previous modern cohort shaped by a strong president. The Founding generation had no political or corporate institutions to rely on in order to see their vision through. They had to create everything from scratch. Guided by their faith in God and their understanding of God's natural law, the Founding Fathers created a nation destined to do great things.

Generation T will fulfill this mission and in so doing, they will shatter the perceived "wisdom" of an America destined to decline while foreign powers rise. Other countries have been beating us because our leadership has let us down. They have made Americans lose faith in their nation and of their individual ability to shape the future.

President Trump has put a stop to such meagre thinking. Generation T is more confident, competent, faithful, and patriotic than their predecessors. In the words of President Trump, "Americanism not globalism is our credo," and so it is with Generation T.

One of the many reasons that so many of liberal men and women of corporate America are turning to President Trump is because they know that future generations will abandon their products and services if they fail to keep up with the ethos of Generation T. By embracing President Trump's leadership, they are signalling a willingness to embrace the values of Generation T for the pragmatic reason that their future customer base, and far more importantly, their future shareholders are members of the generation that came of age under President Trump.

Generation T is already vastly more financially literate than any other generation in American history was in their teens and twenties. The ease with which President Trump is able to describe the realities of leading a board of directors, and the wisdom with which he offers profound micro- and macro-economic insight is not lost on this generation. Generation T hears President Trump's words, and they seek to emulate and internalize this wide reservoir of knowledge.

It is time to prognosticate less and to do more. It is time to move out of a nostalgic bubble and time to make a future worthy of any past. It is time to Make America Great Again. This is President Trump's message, and this is the guiding ethos of Generation T.

Chapter 15

President of the World

When President Trump was first elected, both supporters and opponents struggled to analogize his leadership to that of familiar presidents of the twentieth century. In my book, *Trump and Reagan: Defenders of America*, I detailed how the two highly popular Republicans share a great deal in common, a fact that many Republicans were afraid to make at the time, even though when it comes to success in a Republican White House, this can no longer be denied.

But in many ways, there is another leader to whom President Trump is a natural successor. In the 2024 election cycle and in his second term, President Trump has spoken a great deal about the strong legacy of President William McKinley.

McKinley's legacy suffers from the fact that his administrations commenced prior to the advent of radio and television. Yet in many ways, McKinley was the first truly modern president.

In terms of biography, McKinley's life served as a national link between the final days of the Civil War and Reconstruction era on one hand, and the dawn of the twentieth century on the other. McKinley's 1896 election was one of the most ideologically fraught in history.

McKinley was a firm believer in the gold standard while his charismatic Democrat opponent, William Jennings Bryan, favored monetary bimetallism. Bryan blamed the recession of 1893 on the gold-backed dollar. According to this theory, farmers and working men suffering from a "deflationary crisis" would benefit from a currency backed by both silver and gold. Bryan's impassioned defense of silver did not account for Gresham's law, the economic theory that effectively disproves the supposed benefits of bimetallism by pointing out that "bad money drives out good."

If a national currency is based on two metals (e.g. gold and silver) and the market value of the weaker metal (silver) falls below the prescribed government ratio vis-a-vis gold, the weaker currency will flood the market while the stronger currency (gold) will be hoarded, thus leading to an inflationary crisis which itself results in malinvestment.

While Bryan ran a campaign that criss-crossed the nation, McKinley allowed the people to come to him. Much like President Trump, McKinley took questions from the public and the press every day of the week, apart from Sunday. No presidential candidate interacted with the public at a more direct level before and few have since. President Trump is of course one of those few who have interacted with the public and media more than any previous president.

McKinley's victory represented a pivotal change in the history of electoral politics. This change is often referred to as the Fourth Party System. The era was dominated by the Republican party and McKinley set the tone.

In addition to a classical gold standard that was formally legislated under McKinley, the McKinley White House is also remembered for solving the recession of the early 1890s by collecting tariffs. In the McKinley era, the GDP of the United States continually surpassed that of the British Empire, thus marking the shift in the global epicenter of power from London and Westminster to Wall Street and Washington, DC.

Although the wars of the late twentieth and early twenty-first centuries have been costly while producing no tangible benefits to the United States (whether LBJ's Vietnam, Bush's Iraq, or Obama's Libya), McKinley expanded US territory while the revenue kept pouring in.

McKinley's view of foreign policy was a broad-based conception of Manifest Destiny. It was under McKinley that the United States acquired Hawaii, began the building of the Panama Canal, and took charge of Cuba and the Philippines from the Spanish Empire.

While few cities today can hold an Olympic Games without losing money, McKinley broadened territorial holdings outside the Continental United States, all the while a booming economy allowed innovation to proceed at a hitherto unknown pace on the home front.

McKinley was born in the era of the horse and wagon. When he tragically died at the hands of an assassin's bullet in 1901, he left behind a country with electricity, advanced sanitation systems, the best railroads in the world, and the beginnings of recorded sound, the telephone, and the automobile.

McKinley's successor, President Theodore Roosevelt, has been rightly described by President Trump as the inheritor and highly capable custodian of the McKinley legacy. This is not to detract from Roosevelt's greatness, but unlike McKinley who won two convincing elections for his party, Roosevelt ended up splitting the GOP in 1912, thus enabling the victory of the Democrat

Woodrow Wilson—a man who took the nation into a very un-McKinleyesque First World War.

Many of our recent presidents seem both financially illiterate and geopolitically disloyal when compared to both President McKinley and President Trump. The McKinley/Trump conception of foreign policy is one where the president's duty is to fight for the best interests of his country through tough negotiations with all other nations. This is true whether such nations are formal adversaries or those with similar cultures and foundations.

The contrast between this style of leadership and that of every other twenty-first-century president could not be more stark. The other US presidents of the twenty-first century tended to see foreign policy as a game in which the US was merely a player in a wider team. George W. Bush, Barack Obama, and Joe Biden (or whoever was in charge during his single term) did not distinguish between the interests of the European Union, United Nations, World Trade Organization, Canada, Mexico, and the US itself.

For these men, the US was the equivalent of an uninspired quarterback whose job was to manage the game. Making matters worse, these same leaders treated our adversaries with a combination of contempt and subterfuge. This is the surefire way of getting absolutely nothing done.

By contrast, Presidents McKinley and Trump enter negotiations with any and every foreign entity with the same spirit of putting America First. They do so, safe in the knowledge that the other countries are entering the negotiation with the same mentality regarding their countries' best interests. In terms of adversarial nations, both men were honest. They let their position be known and offered the other countries a chance to negotiate from a rational point of view or otherwise "take or leave" what was on the table.

This is the time-tested recipe for success in foreign affairs. China does not see itself as a member of a team, it sees itself as the leading power of Asia and one of the economic power houses of the modern world. Russia doesn't see itself as an equal to the members of its supposed CIS alliance, but instead sees itself as the master of the regions it borders. The EU, perhaps the most disingenuous of all, pretends that it is a team player, but does everything it can to make doing business in its borders impossible—more so if your company is from America, less so if it is from China.

While other presidents pretended not to see these facts that are as clear as day, Trump not only sees them but regularly talks about them. His cards are on the table. If you want to do business with the US, which every country in the world does, the US will not roll over and sell out its interests—not under President Trump, just as this was the case with President McKinley.

Those who have been indoctrinated into thinking that peace springs from weakness, may be surprised to learn that McKinley and Trump were both peace presidents. It seems perplexing, but many on the left argued that President Trump would cause a third world war upon taking office for the first time. These same people then opposed all of President Trump's plans for peace, although they were not ultimately able to derail them.

One of President Trump's most remarkable peace-making moments came on the Demilitarized Zone (DMZ) on the Korean Peninsula. While American social media is not available in North Korea, President Trump declared a Twitter War on the country and its leader Kim Jong-un in 2017. Using official government statements, Kim fired back in a bloodless battle that kept some on edge, while amusing many others.

The result was neither war nor stalemate. The result was hitherto unimaginable peace and friendship. President Trump's historic Singapore Summit with Kim Jong-un represented the first meaningful thaw in Korean tensions since an uncomfortable armistice ended the hot phase of the Korean War in 1953.

In 2019, President Trump became the first sitting president to step foot on North Korean soil. The moment was not planned by either side. It came amid a peace summit on the South Korean side of the border. In a moment that changed the tide of human history, Kim Jong-un extended his hand to President Trump and invited him to walk with him across the border, into the North. Both smiled as they took one small step for two men and one giant leap for the peace of mankind. So much for World War Three!

But President Trump was not finished. After decades of wasteful wars in the Middle East which resulted in the creation of a demonic terror group called ISIS (a name that Obama refused to say), President Trump pivoted US policy from one of costly foolishness to one of rapidly destroying ISIS while drastically reducing troop levels and financial commitments to the fraught region. This was yet another major success.

President Trump also helped to normalize relations among multiple powers of the wider Middle Eastern region. The Abraham Accords set in motion a historic era of peace between the wealthiest states of the Arab world and Israel. Had the cooked election of 2020 not happened, full-scale Middle Eastern peace would have been not only possible, but likely by 2021. Think of all the thousands of people who are now dead, who would otherwise be alive, if President Trump was allowed to get on with the business of peacemaking before a rude interruption of four years.

Central to President Trump's peacemaking is his humanity. Have you ever listened to your average politician speak and asked yourself, "Is this guy for real?" If you speak in riddles in public, you'll have a hard time winning trust in private. By contrast,

President Trump speaks the same way in public as he does in private. He is straightforward, highly informed, unwilling to water down his positions, but nevertheless, he is an incredibly warm human being.

The tough leaders of major powers respect this. What they do not respect is the "community organizer," or worse yet "left wing DEI" rhetoric of some of the other American politicians who aspire to "leadership." When President Trump talks about how foreign powers laughed at us under his predecessors, he is not exaggerating.

The great military philosopher Sun Tzu said, "If you know the enemy and know yourself you need not fear the results of a hundred battles." This encapsulates President Trump's negotiating strategy whether with New York officials about a building project or with the leaders of China and Russia.

Another element of President Trump's character that is widely respected globally is his warmth. As an Elvis fan, President Trump knows that "we can't go on together with suspicious minds." If there is no level of basic human trust that can be formed or otherwise ascertained at the commencing of negotiations, nothing meaningful can get done.

President Trump respects all of his global counterparts so long as they respect the United States. He has no ideological or personal axe to grind with others. He simply wants to get things done and prefers to do so in a way that leaves everyone walking away with a sense of contentment. If President Trump had less lofty ambitions in life and sought to be a legal mediator, he would have been the most skilled in his field. A smile costs the same price as a grimace, but it pays dividends when it comes to getting things done.

While others confuse toughness with grimness, President Trump clearly demonstrates just how different these traits are. In his second Inaugural Address, President Trump laid out the clear and fundamental truth behind a sound foreign policy:

> From this day forward, our country will flourish and be respected again all over the world. We will be the envy of every nation, and we will not allow ourselves to be taken advantage of any longer. During every single day of the Trump administration, I will, very simply, put America first.

President Mckinley would be proud.

Chapter 16

Trump and Free Speech: My Mission to Make Trumpism Permanent

If people listen closely, they will notice that President Trump never talks about apocalyptic themes. The Bush era and Obama era attempted to recast politics in absolute terms. All this served to do was absolutely disappoint all sides. By contrast, President Trump sees all problems mathematically and every math problem has a solution if the person trying to solve it is smart enough.

This is the essence of Trumpism—it is fundamentally about problem solving. Whether in business or in politics, the only way to actually accomplish something practical is to think in this way. Any other methodology is doomed to overpromise and critically, to underdeliver.

The problem of censorship has always been one that is close to my heart. While worries about censorship have always been central to my own political agenda of supporting and expanding constitutional liberties, I could never have imagined that I would live to see *any* president of the United States wholesale censored.

In an early chapter, I discussed how it felt watching President Trump censored in real time in January 2021. It was Orwellian, communistic, and most of all, it was incredibly un-American.

There is no greater privilege in my life than being an American. While some are blessed by God to be born in this great nation, I made my path to this shining city on a hill. I love everything about the United States, but perhaps most of all, I love the First Amendment. As someone who has dedicated his life to political activism and advisory positions in the Trump campaign and Trump White House, as well as being an author, educator, and speaker, my entire life has been literally made possible by the First Amendment.

In my birth nation of Australia, politics, speaking, writing, and education exist, but they do so under a cloud of fear. This is because arbitrary, politicized, and downright cynical censorship from the top down can occur at any moment. It is immoral, but there, it is legal. Fortunately for the United States, the First Amendment is a bulwark against the kinds of censorship that are a regular occurrence throughout the world, whether in one-party dictatorships or supposed democracies that have decided to traverse the slippery slope to tyranny through the back door.

On his first day back in office in 2025, President Trump signed a powerful executive order to force all arms of the federal government to cease their censorship activities, including but not limited to the direct coercion of tech companies in the pursuit of stifling the constitutional rights of Americans, up to and including the president himself.

However, many dangers remain for one simple reason. President Trump's final term will end in 2029. While many if not most of his supporters would want him to seek a further term, this is unlikely to happen, even though I suspect that if the 22nd Amendment was repealed, President Trump would win a third term by a larger margin than FDR did in 1940.

Supporters of President Trump owe it to ourselves to do everything we can to assure that his legacy in government is locked-in so that Generation T is able to move forward and carry this legacy forward. It was shortly after President Trump's re-election that I decided to do something to prevent any future president from weakening the free speech protections installed by President Trump.

To understand the importance of a permanent buttress against the increasingly censorious left, it is important to understand how our free speech rights were not handed down to us with ease. Instead, our Founding Fathers had to "fight, fight, fight" to give Americans the fundamental freedoms that far too many still take for granted.

All patriotic Americans are familiar with the greatest fight for freedom in human history that took place between 1776 and 1783. Our Revolutionary War was a clarion call to free people to throw off the shackles of tyranny, not in the name of anarchy but in the name of God's own natural law. A less familiar story, but an equally important one, is the struggle to realize this great revolutionary spirit in the lives of men and women who had turned their swords to plowshares.

The 1962 movie, *Lawrence of Arabia*, contains a line of dialog that ought to inform any study of peacemaking and of governing itself:

> *Young men make wars—and the virtues of war are the virtues of young men—courage and hope for the future. And then old*

men make the peace, and the vices of peace are the vices of old men—mistrust and caution.

Such words would have offered wise counsel to our Founding Fathers who spent much of the late 1780s determining the nature of government in a new nation.

Our first attempt at establishing a peacetime government came in the form of the Articles of Confederation. This document, ratified in 1781, guaranteed the freedom of the original thirteen states whose citizens had fought so valiantly in the Revolution. But while the articles guaranteed freedom among the states, there was no plan for how to manage the struggling economies of the states. As a result, a young nation floundered and was on the verge of failure. A real danger of conquest from a foreign power seemed imminent.

Ever the inventive nation, a solution was reached. Under the tutelage of James Madison, our Constitution was drafted and ratified in June 1788. But this was not the end of the disquiet. While the Constitution ensured effective and fair governance, many citizens of the states believed that the Constitution was an insufficient restraint on government's propensity to infringe on the liberties of the individual.

And thus, a solution that has inspired free men and women throughout the world was reached. Our Constitution was amended ten times, becoming the Bill of Rights.

First among these amendments were the words that set the United States most poignantly apart from all other nations:

> Congress shall make no law respecting an establishment of religion, or prohibiting the free exercise thereof; or abridging the freedom of speech, or of the press; or the

right of the people peaceably to assemble, and to petition the Government for a redress of grievances.

With these profound words, it was made clear that under God's natural law, our ability to speak without the fear of censorship could not be infringed by government.

But this was not the end of the story.

In the twenty-first century, elected officials and bureaucrats at a federal and state level developed a resentment of both the letter and spirit of the First Amendment. Making matters worse for those who wish to live under the letter and spirit of the First Amendment, is the fact that censorious proxies in the private sector have taken it upon themselves to censor and severely punish Americans who simply wish to enjoy their God-given rights.

The Censorship Industrial Complex has many vectors that function in a manner that is frighteningly analogous to China's infamous Social Credit System. Under the Biden administration, the federal government worked to actively coerce major corporations into the censorship of citizens attempting to enjoy the rights guaranteed by the Constitution.

But this is only the tip of the iceberg. While President Trump has signed an executive order mandating the total cessation of government directed censorship, there remain major problems that can only be dealt with through legislation that will permanently exorcise the un-American Censorship Industrial Complex in all of its many forms.

Under the Biden administration, the Censorship Industrial Complex functioned as a direct pipeline through which the federal government ordered the censorship of Americans. Shortly before President Trump's second inauguration, Meta CEO Mark Zuckerberg told Joe Rogan that Biden administration officials often screamed and swore at Meta executives when they felt that the censorship orders were not being heeded in an expeditious manner.

But the Censorship Industrial Complex predates the dark years of the Biden administration. Prior to 2021, the Censorship Industrial Complex was a highly advanced web of foreign interests, foreign money, and even foreign governments that exerted influence on American companies. Their goal was not just to stop Americans from exercising their First Amendment Rights, their goal was to ruin American lives.

Funds from foreign governments and independent financiers from across the world pay for the founding of spurious "thank tanks" and "watchdog" groups. Many of these groups are based abroad, some with US subsidiaries, while some are based in the US. These groups produce reports which claim that American men and women exercising their constitutional rights are somehow "dangerous" individuals. But the work of these groups does not end with slander.

The work of these otherwise obscure groups is then amplified by major left-leaning media outlets in both the US and overseas. These reports are then used by major tech platforms as the excuse to censor the voices of Americans, most of whom are patriotic, most of whom are telling the truth, but all of whom have one important thing in common—their speech is protected by the First Amendment.

The story does not end there. Following the censorship, many of the censored individuals find themselves banned from important financial service providers including major banks and online apps such as PayPal and Venmo. This process has become so frighteningly common that the neologism "debanking" has entered the lexicon to denote this shocking phenomenon. The process has been discussed by leading public figures including President Trump, Elon Musk, Tucker Carlson, Vivek Ramaswamy, Marc Andreessen, Joe Rogan, Ron Paul, and many others.

After being banned from access to key financial services, such individuals then find themselves banned from using the services of hotels/property rentals (including Airbnb), ride services including Uber and Lyft, and even food delivery apps. The goal is to send a message to others who might have otherwise decided to challenge corporate or political authority in the way that the heroes of 1776 did. The message is clear: sit down, shut up, and do as you are told. There is no more un-American message in the world.

To be clear, the individuals and groups who have been censored, debanked, and "de-serviced" have not committed any crime. They have not been accused of doing so. Their record is clean and yet their lives are ruined. Although this can and has happened to Americans of many ideological backgrounds, an overwhelming number of those facing these problems are Christian conservatives.

The realities outlined above might seem totally alien to Americans who have been sheltered from these horrors. But in China, the description of censorship, debanking, and deservicing, would be very familiar. For many years, China has operated what is known as a "social credit system." Using the country's highly integrated and largely government-controlled tech sector, the public and private conversations that Chinese citizens have are all monitored by high tech algorithms. When something is said that is met with disapprobation by the Chinese state, such people find that while they have money in their bank account, they cannot access it. While they have purchased a ticket for a plane or train, they are not allowed to travel. Some are even prevented from marrying due to having a poor social credit score.

The essence of the Chinese social credit score is already here.

It existed before Biden, it was perfected during Biden, and there were no plans to stop it prior to President Trump's signature hitting an executive order, which prohibits federal agencies from doing what they perfected under Biden and Harris.

With all of this in mind, I started an organization to not only secure President Trump's free speech legacy, but to prevent Americans exercising their constitutional rights from facing political or private sector retribution ever again. I call my group **1A Warriors**. It is built around finding straightforward, practical, and generationally secure solutions to the complex problems intentionally created by the left. I could not have formed such a group without the wisdom I learned from *The Art of The Deal* when I first read it in 1998.

For decades, the left has excelled at legislating their priorities into a state of unshakable permanency. They have excelled at this because when in power, the left is far less naive than conservatives. Conservatives have relied too much on elections and too little on institutional and legislative capture when it comes to advancing our priorities.

The left does this by authorizing legislation that first enshrines their grievances into law. Then, they use the media, culture, the arts, and sports to promote the ethos of their legislation. Once this is done, a generation of Americans comes to accept leftist ideology as part of the social fabric. Finally, for decades after a piece of legislation is passed, the left uses multiple non-profit groups to litigate any challenges to this legislation into oblivion.

With few exceptions, the right has totally failed to grasp the success that the left has had in their methods. But there are some examples. Between the 1960s and the present day, there is one specific area in which conservatives have expanded our liberties. This area is our right to keep and bear arms. Across multiple presidents and congresses and across the majority of all states, the right to exercise our constitutional right to keep and bear arms has expanded. How did conservatives do this?

Conservatives did this by forming organized, intelligent, and disciplined groups that pursued legislative action, lobbying, public outreach, education, media content creation, litigation, and electioneering to ensure that from top to bottom, our Second Amendment would not be infringed, irrespective of which party was in power at which level of government.

1A Warriors will do for the First Amendment what other conservative groups have done for the Second Amendment. Our fundamental solution lies in using existing civil rights legislation to do for conservatives and Christians exactly what the Left has done for its core constituents for over fifty years. To understand this solution, one must explore arguments over the Fourteenth Amendment that occurred in Congress during the 1960s.

The Fourteenth Amendment establishes equal protection for all citizens under the law. In many ways, the Fourteenth Amendment confided *de facto* what had been implied *de jure* in earlier amendments to the Constitution. However, in keeping with President Lincoln's vision for an emancipated Union, Republicans made the decision to make equality an explicit fact of constitutional law.

This was done in the form of the comprehensive legislation that became the Civil Rights Act of 1964. One of the more controversial parts of this legislation at the time was Title II of the Act. Title II delineates the prohibition of discrimination against protected classes within the realm of "public accommodations." The term "public accommodations" is herein defined to include all major privately owned establishments that are accessible to the public on a transactional basis.

Because Title II dealt with privately owned facilities that

served as "public accommodation," this was the most widely challenged part of the Civil Rights Act by its opponents. Ultimately, the Supreme Court ruled that Title II was constitutional in a case known as *Heart of Atlanta Motel v. United States* in 1964.

Title II is not going anywhere, and therefore, the solution is not to relitigate the past but instead, to use a piece of legislation that is a permanent part of our legal landscape in order to afford rights to one of the few groups who remain unprotected by *any* civil rights legislation.

It became evident that an amendment to the Civil Rights Act was necessary to include a new protected class. This class would be expansively defined to encompass individuals participating in public speech, the expression of viewpoints, or activism that is safeguarded by the First Amendment.

With this in place, not only would those exercising their First Amendment rights be protected from censorship, but all forms of retribution designed to ruin one's existence and chill the future exercising of First Amendment rights would be brought to an end. Implicit in this solution, as is the case with any solution looking to safeguard President Trump's ongoing accomplishments, is creativity. This is a further reason underlying the widespread popularity of President Trump.

Prior to President Trump, creativity in politics was viewed as a liability. Among President Trump's opponents it still is. Nobody wanted to rock the boat, they were instead focused on tricking the public so that they wouldn't notice that prior to President Trump, the country was lilting like a sinking ship.

I remember vividly, during the 2016 campaign, when President Trump explained that one of the reasons we were getting killed on trade by China, is because their negotiators and trade officials were smart while the American officials of the Obama era (and before) were stupid. In speaking this undeniable truth, President Trump threw down the gauntlet for a new way of thinking—a new way of problem solving.

Of course, President Trump did far more than expose the failures of the pre-Trump era. His solutions are creative, inventive, and aimed at getting deals done, not having important matters left unsettled. We saw this in the way in which President Trump saved access to TikTok for millions of Americans. While Sleepy Joe in all his uncreative ignorance said, "ban or sell," President Trump proposed a deal and got it done.

It is imperative for President Trump's supporters to learn from the man who changed America. We must never go back. Instead, we must legislate and litigate President Trump's legacy into the fabric of America.

1A Warriors will do its part, and my hope is that those reading this book, those listening to President Trump's speeches, and those reading *The Art of The Deal* will learn these valuable lessons.

President Trump is a teacher as much as he is a leader. It is our time to do all we can to keep up the good work even though his 2025–2029 term is likely President Trump's grand finale.

Chapter 17

From TDS to DT Yes!

As someone who supported President Trump from the moment he and Melania came down from the top of Trump Tower to greet the world as a future President and First Lady, I have observed the strange financial, sociological, and party political expressions of the disease known as "Trump Derangement Syndrome" or TDS.

To reiterate, prior to his decision to run for President as a Republican, President Trump was one of the most beloved men in the country. In the words of Kipling, he was (and remains) a man who can "Walk with kings nor lose the common touch." He was the "people's billionaire," the man who was neither a hermetic and grimacing Mr. Burns stereotype, nor was he the try-hard type who pretends to be "just a regular guy." President Trump has always been larger than life, but he has always been someone whose feet are on the ground. Whether speaking with the kings, premiers, and presidents of foreign countries, doing the biggest business deals of the era, or chatting with a construction worker, voter, or golfer, President Trump is who he is: an honest man who respects you unless you give him a very good reason not to do so.

How then was such a beloved man turned into the media's "public enemy number one"? The answer is simple: it takes money, lots of it. TDS was not a naturally occurring virus, it was made in the well-funded labs of a legacy media that was already on its last legs, but got a shot in the arm when powerful forces commanded them to wage the most costly and wide reaching propaganda campaign in history.

The moment it became clear that President Trump was serious about implementing an America First agenda and ending the cult of globalism, corporate money and funds from sinister "NGOs" from abroad began pouring into the ecosystem of both legacy and online media. The disease was less about objectively convincing people of that which was objectively untrue, but rather to sow fear. Specifically, they sought to make people literally afraid of expressing their admiration for and support of President Trump in both public and private.

The methods were not dissimilar to that of secret police forces in the communist regimes that fell in the aftermath of President Reagan's second term. Logically, the residents of communist states knew that it was impossible for half the population to be members of the secret police. But because of the fact that membership of the secret police was not disclosed to the public, ordinary people were afraid to speak their minds even in private due to the fear that their neighbor, friend, coworker, or stranger on the bench might be an informant for the secret police.

Likewise, the super-spreaders of TDS wanted every American to fear that the men or women to whom they would express support for President Trump were part of a network that would socially and financially ostracize them due to their positive opinion on President Trump. This is one of the reasons that professional pollsters failed to predict the size and scope of President

Trump's victory. So conditioned were members of the public to conceal their support for President Trump, that they did not even trust anonymous pollsters with their "secret."

These techniques did not just mimic those of communist regimes. They were literally taken from the communist playbook of the twentieth century. To understand how the super-spreaders of TDS borrowed from previously classified communist propaganda techniques, one must revisit the words of Yuri Bezmenov.

Bezmenov was a high ranking official in the KGB of the Soviet Union. He was a communist and worked with others to infiltrate the American education system in order to break the minds of our youth. We know this because Bezmenov developed a conscience against tremendous odds. This conscience led him to seek refuge in the United States where he sought to tell his story. Few at the time were interested, but one man was.

In 1984, of all years, journalist and author G. Edward Griffin used his own money to assemble a camera crew to interview Bezmenov about how the communists, how the radical left, sought to undermine our young men's minds. The repentant communist said that the key to destroying a country is through the demoralization of its youth and its young men in particular. Bezmenov said that a demoralized person would not even recognize the truth if it was clearly presented to them.

This is creepy but it is not science fiction. When we are told that men can get pregnant and women can wave their very male organ around in a locker room, this isn't just weird, it is part of a calculated plan to make America weak by demoralizing us. Once demoralized, we will lose our will to be great because we will lose our ability to understand natural law—the same natural law on which our Constitution is based.

This was their method of attacking President Trump. Some

knew what they were doing, others were paid for it, others were what Bezmenov reminded Griffin and referred to as "useful idiots." These were the "true believers"—individuals who drank the communist kool aid only to find that when their "comrades" took power, things did not turn out as promised.

The fact that all of this was going on simultaneous to the censorship discussed in the previous chapter, paints a very grim picture of reality in the land of the free. But there is fortunately more to the story. In true American fashion, if the existing business model was failing to deliver, enterprising Americans simply invented a new one. The more that legacy media became the propaganda organs infecting the world with TDS, free speakers of all varieties flooded to the free spaces of social media.

In the 2024 cycle, this included Truth Social, X, Rumble, and the wider world of podcasts that could be spread across multiple platforms with ease. From comedians and athletes to businessmen and union members and housewives, everyone who could operate even the most basic smartphone or computer could now hear the *authentic* voice of America. Unsurprisingly, the vast majority of people who abandoned the legacy media were supporters of President Trump.

Even prior to Elon Musk transforming the censorious Twitter into free speech X, I always admired how online social media polls on Twitter and similar platforms always showed huge majorities for President Trump whether he was up against Hillary Clinton, Joe Biden, or Kamala Harris.

These informal polls turned out to predict President Trump's election day successes far more accurately than the results published by professional pollsters. In the social media age, the phrase "touch grass" has entered the lexicon. It means that if you are chronically online, and as a result, your views are shaped solely by internet discourse, you should "go out into the real world" and see what people say and do face-to-face.

As a Trump campaign surrogate, bundler, and regular speaker from coast-to-coast, I interacted with thousands of voters during the campaign. As a result, I was deeply aware that after "touching grass," the social media polls that reflected an overwhelming level of support for President Trump compared to that of his opponents, were absolutely accurate.

Raising over $2 million for President Trump during the campaign felt like a unique moment where we were not just giving to a cause in which we believed, but moreover, we were investing in our own future. This was a source of pride, inspiration, and assurance simultaneously.

In many ways, the collective sentiment in the country shifted dramatically between 2023 and 2024. While President Trump's support was solid in 2023, both on the ground and real life, the last remnants of TDS still prohibited some from declaring their support unless they were certain that they were in the company of compatriots.

As time wore on, the media's lies became so big that a bubble burst. Between the inflation, out of control crime, the abolition of our southern border, the destruction of our industries through a combination of regulation, bad trade policy, and the insistence on DEI, people knew that the media's tricks to demoralize us against our better judgement could no longer work as they once did. To put it another way, the lying media could not demoralize us anymore than Joe Biden did with his policies.

This reality check also helped people to ignore those who continued to spread TDS. Because of this, irrespective of what polling numbers from the "professionals" said about the race being tight, it was clear that the more important question was "just how big will President Trump's victory be?"

The last gasps of TDS were heaved during President Trump's debate with Joe Biden in June 2024. Biden's performance was so incoherent that the legacy media safely retreated up its own ass. They could no longer pretend that it was "insanely conspiratorial" to suggest that Biden's cognition was somewhere between Einstein and Nikola Tesla. In the weeks following Biden's debate farce, something unspeakably horrifying occurred.

It was a sunny day in Butler, Pennsylvania. Tens of thousands of President Trump's supporters filled out a large field where they would hear him speak at one of his legendary rallies—the largest such rallies in American political history. Everything was proceeding as normal when President Trump pointed to a chart on the large screens that demonstrated just how bad the border situation got under Biden.

Suddenly, multiple gunshots rang out. President Trump grabbed his ear before being wrestled to the ground by Secret Service agents. Moments later, he emerged, face covered in blood.

Multiple Secret Service agents attempted to cover President Trump while rushing him off stage, but he would not be hurried. With a face still covered in blood, President Trump looked directly at the crowd, pumped his fist and shouted "fight, fight, fight."

As the world watched this unfold from the many camera angles that documented the attempted assassination, something else unfolded. Many Americans who had been infected with TDS for years, suddenly became immunized.

To see President Trump heroically stare death in the face and emerge stronger than ever had the effect of putting "silent Trump supporters" to shame. Here was a man willing to give his life for his country and there you are, in the safety of your home, afraid to tell your friends that you love President Trump? This is where the demoralization ended. We were now a Trump nation.

There was only one industry where this change was not immediate.

Rather than admit that President Trump's victory was inevitable, the legacy media attempted to hide the story of President Trump's brush with death and instead, rushed to distance themselves from Biden's moribund campaign. They expected the public for forget the previous three years when we were told that nothing was wrong with our Sleepy Crook In Chief.

It didn't work. Their credibility was shot. With that in mind, they pivoted what remained of their propaganda skills to build up the deeply unpopular vice president as the next great leader who would "crush Trump." Outside of legacy media and some polls from the usual suspects, this narrative was never believable.

While Harris was nearly half the age of Biden, she was even less inclined to face the public than Biden. Her appearances were all scripted. Her rallies were opportunities to chant slogans while celebrities shook their rear ends to the music. It was low political theater that went nowhere.

Election day of 2024 was one of those days where you could feel a great historic movement sweeping the country. There were naturally times, early in the day, when I was nervous. Unless you're Joe Namath, you never go into a game thinking that there is a 0 percent possibility that the other team might win. This was particularly true of an election in twenty-first-century America.

After the 2020 debacle, not only did President Trump need to win, he needed a landslide. He needed a victory that was "too big to rig." As the afternoon rolled into evening, I observed as thousands of young men, the kinds of people I had registered to vote during 2023 and 2024, flooded the polls across the country.

Then, one-by-one, it happened. Not one, not two, but all seven swing states went to President Trump. Every single county in the nation pivoted closer to President Trump. Because of President Trump's leadership, Republicans expanded their majority in the House and won back the Senate.

It was well and truly a new dawn at the precipice of a new golden age.

Chapter 18

Trump's Effect on the Left

Earlier, it was explained how in a Faustian gamble for short-term gain, the Obama-era Democrats killed off their traditional base and replaced this with an urbane constituency whose politics consist entirely of those with sexual and racial grievances. What the Democrats did not expect, however, was the departure of their *old* base to a new party.

What the Democrat strategists behind this pivot did not account for is that a Republican would ever come along who was intelligent enough to speak directly to the politically homeless labor union members, blue collar workers, and young men, among others.

The Clinton era began to see a growing schism among Roman Catholic voters who had voted overwhelmingly Democrat prior to Clinton's quiet (and sometimes not so quiet) embrace of the pro-abortion movement. When this was compounded by a loss of blue-collar workers, the Democrats reverted to what they were during the Reconstruction era. They became a party defined by the social grievances of regionalism rather than a party with a clear set of constituents on the left and center in all fifty states.

This time however, the Democrats weren't the party of the South, but the party of large coastal cities with a smattering of cities in the Midwest, namely Chicago. The 2024 electoral county map showed that *even* in blue counties in blue states, there was a pivot away from Democrats to Republicans. Making matters worse for the Democrats is that for the first time in modern history, the second Trump administration is committed to removing the trans-administrational Democrat machinery from our federal bureaucracy.

Even though Democrats have been slowly alienating their traditional base for years, they were able to rely on bloated and wasteful federal departments, agencies, and sub-agencies to do their bidding in such a way that sabotaged the electoral promises of Republicans in both the executive and legislative branches.

President Trump's creation of the Department of Government Efficiency (DOGE), his executive orders ending the Democrat installed DEI programs throughout federal agencies, the arrival of Robert F. Kennedy Jr. at the Department of Health and Human Services, border czar Tom Holman, and other major reformers, all represent a new approach to getting bureaucracy under control. Removing the trap doors that Democrats have stealthily built in the federal bureaucracy for over a century is a huge component of President Trump's legacy. It is one that the Democrats have not even begun to fully grasp, at least not in public.

With former Democrat voting blocs turning to President Trump and his party at the ballot box, and with the federal bureaucracy hollowed of its Democrat cobwebs, the Democrats may well be doing some soul searching. It turns out they are not.

The Democrats have instead retreated to their coastal fortresses with the only group of powerful allies they have left—lawyers. Many suspect that leftist California Governor Gavin

Newsom will lead the Democrats nationally in 2028. Because of this, California's strange brand of politics should not be dismissed as an anomaly.

While much of Los Angeles county was still burning to the ground, Newsom called a special session of his state's legislature to "Trump proof" California. Not long after, the first of many lawsuits was filed by California's attorney general against the White House. No prizes for guessing that this lawsuit was in defense of a legal loophole that had for years been exploited by illegal aliens.

The subject of illegal aliens is also central to this narrative. There is no way to know just how many illegal aliens were allowed into the United States under the Biden/Harris open border, but some estimate the number to be over ten million. During the 2024 cycle, Elon Musk warned that the goal of the Democrats is to give legal status to the illegal aliens when back in power, in order to pave the way for a new group of natural Democrat constituents who would, in the words of Musk, turn the entire country into California.

If anyone wondered why so many Democrats seem to harbor a strange passion for defending convicted murderers and rapists who broke into the country illegally, this is your answer. When you have alienated your traditional core voter base, you have to import one.

The Democrat fanaticism over illegal aliens has only been augmented by the fact that under President Trump, more naturalized citizens who came to the country legally are voting Republican. To become a naturalized citizen after immigrating legally, often takes a lot of time and even more money.

Those who worked hard to become Americans found that the Democrats "welcomed them" by taking their earnings away in the form of punitive taxation. They stifle their ability to run businesses without mind-blowing insane regulation, and they ruin great American cities by unleashing out of control crime. The natural place for anyone with common sense is President Trump's Republican party. Naturalized Americans know this and the Democrats know it too. This does not excuse their deeply immoral strategy, but it does help to explain the rationale of Democrat strategists.

CHAPTER 19

MAGA Meets MAHA

Turning back to the 2024 election itself, a further political revolution took place that many on the left and right have failed to recognize in terms of its size and scope. Just as Republican opposition to high taxation universally resonates with most Democrat voters, Democrat rhetoric on the cost of health care also tends to resonate across party lines for the same reason—both are matters of meat and potatoes realities in household finance.

Enter Robert F. Kennedy Jr., a former Democrat who represented the era when the Democrats had a big political tent. The Kennedy family in particular were very different from today's Democrats. They were stridently anti-communist, unabashedly on the side of the man and woman of strong religious convictions, and they were genuine about delivering a prosperous economy for all Americans.

This is why President Kennedy won the 1960 election and why Robert F. Kennedy would have likely won in 1968, had his life not been cut off by an assassin's bullet.

During the Covid era, RFK Jr. found himself regularly censored by all of the major social media platforms. This was just before the era of Truth Social, X, and the explosion of Rumble. Subsequent evidence in major free speech litigation revealed that in his first forty-eight hours in office, Biden's administration directly ordered the censorship of Kennedy's constitutionally protected speech by social media operators.

In 2023, Kennedy declared that he would challenge Biden in the primaries of the Democrat party in the 2024 election cycle. When Kennedy made this announcement, he made it clear that facing censorship was one of the motivations for his decision to challenge a sitting president from the party with which his family had been associated for over a century. Of course, the primary was openly rigged against Kennedy, which led him to make the decision to run as an independent in October 2023. The Democrats, having successfully driven Kennedy out of the party, then filed numerous lawsuits to keep Kennedy off the ballot as an Independent. While they ignored Kennedy in public, in private their actions revealed a deep fear.

By the summer of 2024, Kennedy was ready to make an announcement for the ages. He decided to withdraw from the race to join forces with President Trump. Kennedy, who was always beloved among MAGA, became an instant hero to President Trump's supporters, who had become ever more health conscious.

For the young men following conservative commentators like myself, and those following the world's major podcasts, notably Joe Rogan's, the issues of personal fitness, nutrition, and health had become a front and center issue. Young men in the MAGA movement were avoiding toxic processed foods in favor of locally hunted venison and organic juicy steaks. They weren't taking drugs but taking vitamins. They weren't hanging out at the malls that closed under Biden, they were hanging out at the gym.

Because health was the major focus of Kennedy's campaign and a lifelong passion, he became the perfect political symbol for many of the young men who were naturally drawn to both President Trump's message of MAGA and Kennedy's message of MAHA—Make America Healthy Again.

Beyond this, there was something symbolic in seeing President Trump, a political outsider who defined an era, embracing the son of Senator Robert F. Kennedy who, along with President Kennedy, came to define the optimistic side of the 1960s, a decade whose dark undertones resulted in large part from the tragic demise of both towering figures.

Politically, the Trump-RFK Jr. alliance also represented yet another core issue taken away from the Democrats. While the Democrats of the last forty years never did anything to improve the nation's health, they sure loved talking about it. The relics of the pre-Trump GOP did little to combat this perennial Democrat talking point. While Obamacare objectively made health care more expensive and worse, in one of his final moves on the Senate floor, John McCain gave a thumbs down to President Trump's proposals to reform the Democrats' (Un)Affordable Care Act.

But with Kennedy on board, the narrative had changed. It became clear that the Democrats and pre-Trump GOP did nothing to address the issues of health that my supporters, Joe Rogan's listeners, and millions of social media influencers clearly valued. Now there was an opportunity of a generation to press the reset button on the nation's health. It would not be accomplished through big spending and big bureaucracy, it would be done in the gyms and grocery stores of the nation, as well as by the long overdue reform of Washington's morbidly obese health agencies.

In classic Kennedyesque elegance, RFK Jr. said the following about his endorsement of and partnership with President Trump in the final months of the 2024 campaign:

> For nineteen years, I spent thirty minutes praying every day when I got out of bed, and my prayer was I asked God to put me in a position where I could end the chronic disease epidemic, and bring health back to our children. In August, God sent me Donald Trump.

The political, social, and practical significance of this statement continues to reverberate in the halls of Washington and in the country as a whole.

The Democrats could no longer call themselves the party of health, not that they ever really had a right to do so in recent decades. Around the same time that Kennedy endorsed President Trump, civil libertarian and veteran Tulsi Gabbard joined the GOP and also strongly endorsed President Trump. The few sound minds in the Democrat Party were now on the Trump Train. It was well and truly game over for the party of Gavin Newsom and Nancy Pelosi.

When he declared his candidacy in 2015, President Trump said that he would be able to bring new voters into his party and become a universally loved figure, someone who would be a president for the full nation—someone like Presidents Kennedy and Reagan.

After fighting an eight-year war with the media and against the sadistic lawfare of the DNC, President Trump's vision was coming to fruition.

As someone who was always on President Trump's side, perhaps the best advice I could give anyone in politics is this: Never bet against President Trump. Never scoff at his predictions, never laugh at his ideas and ideals, never try to stop his momentum.

President Trump is a born winner and as he promised, 2024 showed that far from getting tired of winning, MAGA was winning in areas never thought possible before.

Chapter 20

Election Night

Mountains were moved in the months and years leading up to election night on November 5, 2024. I, along with tens of thousands of volunteers throughout the nation, not only worked to get out the vote, but worked to ensure that ordinary voters knew how to vote. Making sure that your vote was counted before leaving a polling station was a must. We could not tolerate, nor could the country withstand, another repeat of the 2020 disaster.

And yet, there was always a lingering suspicion that Democrats and their cronies would once again make it so that a fair outcome was impossible to achieve. There was also a lingering feeling that a speedy vote count would not be "allowed," something which in and of itself is an indication of an intent to cheat.

When the polls began to close on the east coast, there was no way of knowing if it was going to be a long night or a long month. And then it happened. Social media, CNN, Fox, and all the other news channels began lighting up with images of President Trump's face next to the maps of all the vital swing states. He ended up not just winning a sufficient number of swing states, he won them all.

The election proved too big to rig. Our hard work was not in vain, instead he had secured something far more profound than an election victory. We had undone four years of hardship, scandal, inflation, national decline, crime, and pain.

Our four-year national nightmare was over. As the crowd cheered, President Trump said,

> We overcame obstacles that nobody thought possible, and it is now clear that we've achieved the most incredible political thing, look what happened, is this crazy? But it's a political victory that our country has never seen before, nothing like this. I want to thank the American people for the extraordinary honor of being elected your 47th president and your 45th president. And every citizen, I will fight for you, for your family and your future. Every single day I will be fighting for you with every breath in my body, I will not rest until we have delivered the strong, safe and prosperous America that our children deserve and that you deserve. This will truly be the golden age of America, that's what we have to have.

There it was, the declaration of a new golden age for America. The moment we had long awaited, our moment when darkness faded to new light. This was the case because the 2024 election was about far more than replacing a failed leader with one who already had a major record of success.

In fact, 2024 was about replacing a Deep State with a clean state, a cynical attitude of irreversible decline with an optimistic ethos that would see our national exceptionalism restored. It was about waving goodbye to a violent, downtrodden America with one where we could once again see ourselves guided by the timeless virtues of life, liberty, and the pursuit of happiness.

There was something else unique about 2024 compared to 2016. While 2016 was a moment of happiness and pride for President Trump's supporters, it was also when the Democrats, legacy media, the Deep State, foreign "NGOs," and other sinister forces unleashed their plan to hamstring, demoralize, and remove a sitting president just moments after he achieved victory.

From spying on his campaign to using the power of the security state to try to undermine President Trump, 2016 was an electoral victory met with a sinister countercoup that involved hoaxes, censorship, lies, impeachments, and lawfare.

The efforts that were employed to try to destroy President Trump while in office only accelerated and broadened after 2021. But in November 2024, that too appeared to ebb away. It seemed that at long last, many of President Trump's enemies had, at least for the moment, given up on their long campaign of subterfuge. Did the purveyors of impeachment hoaxes, fake lawsuits, fake criminal charges, and two assassination attempts suddenly change their ways? I'm not naive enough to think so.

Instead, it would appear that like an MMA fighter who tries every dirty trick in the book and still loses, the other side was down for the count. They may have had mystery assassins on their side, corrupt judges, and prosecutors, and hysterical media personalities on their side, but President Trump had the most powerful weapon in the world on his side—the trust and support of the great American middle class.

Every rally, every podcast, every speech, and every post on Truth Social had paid off. Business leaders too began to understand just how low the Democrats were willing to sink our economy in order to please their shrinking and shrieking base. Former Democrats from the world of business, ranging from Pershing Square Capital Management's Bill Ackman to Elon Musk and his long-time venture capitalist ally, David Sacks, were all supporting President Trump this time.

Fake narratives about race were gone. President Trump had extended his support among Black, Hispanic, and Asian Americans to record levels while connecting with the white working and middle-class families of the Midwest. Young and old, male and female, coast to coast. This was all MAGA country.

There is an important lesson here that applies equally to life outside of the political arena. While it is not easy to win against those who fight dirty, if you never give up, if you learn to outsmart your opponent, if you grow stronger with every blow they land, and if you keep your faith in God, country, and your own abilities, there is no challenge that cannot be met, no fight that cannot be won, no victory too great to achieve.

This is what President Trump's victory demonstrated on election night. I am confident that this is how it will be remembered for decades and centuries to come.

CHAPTER 21

President Trump's First Letter to the Future

President Trump's second term will leave a profound legacy that will be demonstrated by our future national achievements. Just as President McKinley was born in the age of gaslight and the horse but left office in the age of electricity and the automobile, so too will President Trump be remembered as a man whose life spanned distinct eras of the American experience.

President Trump came of age in a time of boundless energy for our economy, society, and culture. He weathered the storms of national recessions and each time, he presented us with achievements of greatness in the face of adversity. As a businessman, he turned the malaise of the seventies into the renewal of the eighties. Likewise, he weathered the storms of the early nineties to emerge as a national icon in the 2000s.

Following the Great Recession of 2008 and the Obama era of political grievance which followed, he gave us an America that was Made Great Again. The years following 2021 saw President Trump overcome the greatest obstacles ever internationally set before any man, whether in business or in politics. He emerged to deliver us a new Golden Age for America.

By the time President Trump leaves office, I confidently predict that America will have produced hitherto unknowable technological advancements that will dwarf even our most prolific achievements of the past.

Our renewed space program and Space Force will create new frontiers of exploration that will stun even the authors of science fiction.

Our economy will grow while the dollar will remain strong. The United States will be the global capital of a new crypto industry while AI technology will make the chatbots of the early 2020s appear like a horse and carriage attempting to catch a powerful locomotive.

Our suburbs will once again be the safe and happy cradle of a once-again growing middle class. Home ownership will again be attainable for young people, irrespective of their chosen vocation in life.

Our cities will once again become safe places where unique business opportunities and unparalleled cultural greatness are born.

The world will invest in the United States like never before, but our border will be shut to hordes of invaders. We will instead be a nation that welcomes the dreamers, the doers, and the inventors of the world—the best of the best and nothing less.

Our schools will once again teach children both the basics that will help them to thrive in the real world while also providing them the tools with which they can build a better future—a knowledge that they are the next generation in a long line of great Americans stretching from the Pilgrims to the Founding Fathers, from Lincoln to McKinley, from Eisenhower and JFK to Reagan, and from Trump to them.

The alternative would have been unthinkable, but we were very close to long-term Democrat rule that would have resulted in our great suburbs becoming ghettoized favelas, cities becoming Third-World cesspools of drugs, crime, and vice, and our great open country becoming as violent as that of Zimbabwe became when the world stopped looking.

Americans were presented with an opportunity to restore the sheen to our shining city on a hill, or else descend into something worse than civil war. President Trump proved that the good guys don't just win in the movies; they also win in the greatest country on earth, the United States of America.

I have never felt more blessed to live in this country as I do now, to have voted for President Trump, to have campaigned for him, to have registered his voters, to have raised millions of dollars to help We the People attain a priceless goal. But I am one of many. Like the heroes of 1776, times when free men face overwhelming threats are the times when uncommon greatness is thrust upon ordinary patriots from our farms, our cities, our suburbs, our mountains, prairies, and beaches.

One by one, we arose to march against tyranny. Our Republic was restored, greatness was consecrated anew, and a golden future flourished before our eyes.

The movement created by President Trump awakened the great individualistic spirit lying dormant within millions of Americans who had enough and were not going to take it sitting down any longer. We had grown disgusted by spiritual, intellectual, and material weakness, collectivism, the suppression of masculine strength, and the Huxleyan stupefaction of the nation. To be MAGA is to dream big, to do big things, and to forge your own path, alone if necessary, however hard and however long the road to victory may be.

Weeks before he achieved the greatest comeback in American history, President Trump said the following to a packed house at Madison Square Garden:

> I'm here today with a message of hope for all Americans. With your vote in this election, I will end inflation. I will stop the invasion of criminals coming into our country. And I will bring back the American dream. We need the American dream to come back home.
>
> Our country will be bigger, better, bolder, richer, safer and stronger than ever before. This election is a choice between whether we will have four more years of gross incompetence and failure or whether we will begin the four greatest years in the history of our country.
>
> We will achieve success that no one can imagine. We will have the strongest economy, the most secure borders, the safest cities, the most powerful military, the best trade deals, and we will dominate the frontiers of science, medicine, business, technology, and space.
>
> And I'm asking you to be excited about the future of our country again. I'm asking you to dream big again. We're going to dream big again. We haven't been dreaming big at all. This will be America's new golden age.

And so it was that our dreams came true. The American Dream is now our American reality. Ours is a country not just Made Great but Made Greater Than Ever Before.

President Trump never stopped. He never gave up. He fought like hell. He won it all. He did it so that we could have a future that eclipses even the most sublime moments of our most profound dreams.

Thank you, President Trump.

Yours sincerely,

Nick Adams, American

About the Author

Nick Adams is a presidential appointee, four-time bestselling author, motivational speaker, television commentator, and Stage IV cancer survivor. Dubbed a "social media heavyweight" by the *New York Post*, Nick is one of the fastest-growing and furthest-reaching social media influencers in conservative politics, reaching millions every day.

He has appeared on virtually every major television and radio program. He founded and runs the Foundation for Liberty and American Greatness (FLAG), a nonprofit organization that teaches civics and informs parents and students on the power of the American Dream.

Nick served as an official surrogate for the Trump 2024 campaign and developed an election strategy that helped President Trump secure his historic victory.

Three of Nick's bestselling books were endorsed by President Trump during his time in office, leading him to be named "the president's favorite author."